From L...

Michel Syrett is an established business writer, lecturer and researcher. He has written about the developmentof HR policy and practice since the early 1980s. Between 1985 and 1988 he was editor of the quarterly journal of the Institute for Employment Studies, *Manpower Policy and Practice*. He has also written on HR issues for *The Times* (where he was a senior editor for over 10 years), the *Daily Telegraph*, *Financial Times*, *People Management*, *Human Resources*, *Management Today*, *EuroBusiness*, *South China Morning Post*, *Hongkong Standard*, *Asian Business* and the *Economist Intelligence Unit*. As a Visiting Fellow at Cranfield School of Management, he helped to set up what is now the Centre for European Human Resource Management and worked with Professor Andrew Kakabadse conducting research into senior management competencies. He is also a Visiting Professor at the Institut Supérieur des Affaires at Groupe HEC in Paris, where he lectures on strategy and communications, and a Visiting Fellow of the Poon Kam Kai Institute of Management at the University of Hong Kong, where he conducts research into strategic HR issues in Asia. Michel is the author or editor of eight books on business issues.

Jean Lammiman has extensive experience as an HR practitioner, working for companies as varied as Rank Xerox, Bhs and the International Stock Exchange. In the last 10 years she has held a number of important strategic positions in leading blue-chip organisations, including the roles of senior training manager for the International Stock Exchange and director of management development and education at Grand Metropolitan, where (among other things) she was responsible for organisational learning, diversity and senior management development. Jean has also pursued a parallel career as a consultant and academic. She has been a programme director at the City University Business School, where she co-founded the first UK consortium MBA programme, and business development director for ODI, one of the world's leading TQM consultancies. As CEO of the UK business of the international management consultancy the Ambrosetti Group, she also launched a series of programmes, seminars and workshops aimed at CEOs and boardroom directors of blue-chip companies, drawing on a neutral faculty that included many of the world's leading thinkers on business, socio-economic and political trends. Jean is a frequent contributor to conferences on HR issues and has contributed articles to *People Management*, *Human Resources* and the *Journal of Management Development*. She is a Fellow of both the Institute of Personnel and Development and the Institute of Directors.

From Leanness to Fitness

The role of HR in developing corporate muscle

Michel Syrett

and

Jean Lammiman

THE INSTITUTE OF PERSONNEL AND DEVELOPMENT

First published in 1997

Typeset by Wyvern 21 Ltd, Bristol

Printed in Great Britain by
the Cromwell Press, Wiltshire

British Library Cataloguing in Publication Data
A catalogue record for this book is available from the British Library

ISBN 0–85292–685–5

The views expresssed in this book are the authors' own, and may not necessarily reflect those of the IPD.

IPD House, Camp Road, London SW19 4UX
Tel.: 0181 971 9000 Fax: 0181 263 3333

Registered charity no. 1038333. A company limited by guarantee. Registered in England no. 2931892.
Registered office as above.

Contents

To the waterways of Hertfordshire and
our companions on our travels – both were
an inspiration to us in writing this book

Acknowledgements

The unsung heroes of all books are many. Our thanks go to all the senior managers who helped us research the case studies, in particular Christine Gaskell of Rolls-Royce Motor Cars Ltd, Mike Dudding of Kent County Council, Steve French of Birse Construction and Olaf Odlind of Rank Xerox; to our editor Matthew Reisz at the Institute of Personnel and Development for his forbearance; to our business partner Sue, an unfailing source of encouragement and support; and to everyone at home – Johnny, Thomas and Stuart – who performed the kind of everyday interventions that make projects like this possible.

Introduction

Analogy is an extraordinarily potent force in modern life. An academic at one of Europe's top management centres recently commented that effective communication involved the potent use of myths and symbols. Charles Handy has argued, in *The Future of Work* (1985), that to provoke a response in the listener a message should have an 'aha' effect as when everyone says, 'Aha – of course, now I see it.'

So when a team of industrial researchers published a book in 1990 in which they termed new production methods pioneered by Japanese car companies as 'lean' the word struck a chord with a developed world that had recently espoused healthy eating, competitive sport and working out as an ideal. The metaphoric possibilities of health and sport were exploited still further later in the same year by the Harvard professor Rosabeth Moss Kanter in *When Giants Learn to Dance*, where she compared the challenges of running a major corporation to competing in the Olympics.

> Our new heroic model should be an athlete who can manage the amazing feat of doing more with less, who can juggle the need to conserve resources and to pursue growth opportunities. . . . Business athletes need to be intense, lean and limber, able to stretch, and in shape all the time.

The two books unleashed an avalanche of popular business literature extolling the benefits of being lean – a message all too welcome for the many companies, successful as well as unsuccessful, which were engaging in corporate-wide redundancy programmes in order to stay competitive. Suddenly journals and newspapers were full of pictures of fat, puffing and over-bureaucratic corporations being pipped to the contractual post by Moss Kanter-like lean, limber and manifestly delayered companies.

Unfortunately nobody remembered to tell the workforce that being lean was a good thing. The 1996 survey of UK managers by the Institute of Management is typical of many conducted in the mid-

1990s; half the managers surveyed stated that they were overworked and 90 per cent of these stated that the increased stress was affecting both their morale and their effectiveness.

Whenever surveys sought the opinions of employees rather than senior managers the effects of leanness were nearly always painted in a negative light. A 1994 survey of the career implications of delayering by Roffey Park Management Institute found that while staff enjoyed the potential benefits of more autonomy and responsibility they saw this as a threat or a burden leading to overwork, fewer promotion possibilities and greater wastage. In addition little serious work was conducted on the implications of leanness on the HR function other than a spate of articles in 1994 and 1995 on turning the survivors of redundancy programmes into winners.

To rectify this, in June 1995 the Professional Policy Committee of the IPD identified the issue of the lean organisation as a priority for investigation. Prompted by feedback from members that the term leanness was being used to describe a plethora of activities and processes, and for very different ends, the Institute commissioned the Industrial Relations Unit at the University of Warwick and the University of Bath to investigate what might be an appropriate balance between people management policies which allow people to survive and thrive in organisations, giving them adequate scope to develop their full potential, and the need for continual organisational improvement in terms of efficiency and effectiveness.

This book was commissioned separately from the Warwick/Bath research to examine the popular dimensions and issue of leanness. It does not pretend to be an empirical study and the conclusions we have drawn are based on the opinions expressed to us in the six case studies we conducted specifically for this publication. We have also attempted to draw together the existing research and reading on the subject which is summarised in the References.

We have, however, drawn on one aspect of the Warwick/Bath research. In their preliminary report published in 1996 (the completed research was not yet available at the time this book went to print), Professor Purcell and his colleagues at Bath identified three stages of leanness that were common to the organisations they had investigated: leanness as a transitional phase helping the organisation become leaner; leanness as an end-point in itself; and leanness as a process for remaining responsive to market conditions.

We took the Bath findings as the starting-point for our own three-point model. The way in which have used these 'states of existence' is entirely different and the conclusions we have drawn about the role of the HR function are entirely our own. We would like to acknowledge, however, that the Bath report was an inspiration.

Two things struck us most in researching this book. The first is the confusion over the term 'lean'. The MIT research that first coined the term was a comparative study of car manufacturing processes in Japan, North America and Europe. It was commissioned by car manufacturers for manufacturers and it anticipated an audience in industries conducting mass manufacturing. The processes outlined in the book *The Machine That Changed the World* (Womack *et al.*, 1990) – eliminating all unnecessary processes, realigning the remaining processes into a continuous flow, redeploying workers into cross-functional teams and striving for continuous improvement – are not unique to leanness and could equally well apply to a number of other 1990s management doctrines, most notably business process re-engineering and total quality management.

Since we did not wish to aim this book exclusively at large manufacturing companies, we have concentrated on the processes not the term, choosing organisations that have implemented some or all of these in order to illustrate the people management implications. Not all of them use the term 'lean' to describe what they are doing. Whether they are, in fact, lean we will leave the reader to decide.

The second impression we gained is how short a lifespan management doctrines have these days. In a recent lecture Richard Pascale pointed out that spending related specifically to branded doctrines has shot up in the past ten years, creating a whole new industry of academics and consultants that constantly re-invent themselves.

Events have moved on since James Womack and his team at MIT invented leanness. Now the emphasis is on knowledge and value management, organisational learning, creativity and innovation. Employers are keen to espouse a more employee-centred approach to management but they are still working in the economic climate that fostered the lean revolution. In addition it is becoming evident that as we move into the new decade, the doctrine of lean production based on delayered management, horizontal integration and limited outsourcing is going to give way to a more modular structure based on horizontal disintegration, alliances with suppliers and the intensive use of IT.

To this end we have tried to update the concept of leanness by advocating that organisations should be 'fit'. This requires organisations to be able to use the lean structure at their disposal to redeploy resources where they are most needed, investing more in building up the corporate body with the right HR policies. To this end, HR practitioners play a similar role to that of physiologists building muscle in a real athlete.

For what it is worth, this is our contribution to the debate. We hope you enjoy the book.

Michel Syrett
Jean Lammiman
August 1997

1

Leanness: What's in a Name?

To understand the future, you have to understand the past. The problem in looking at the HR implications of leanness is that 'leanness' means different things to different people – and this is a legacy of the piecemeal way it developed as a management concept.

The first question to ask is: is it a management concept at all? Is there sufficient coherence in the way leanness is practised to provide any common ground for developing good HR practice? The answer is only a partial yes. Leanness as a term originated with the publication in 1990 of a piece of MIT research conducted in the late 1980s by a team led by James Womack entitled *The Machine That Changed the World* (Womack *et al.*, 1990). Conducted over five years by a team of international academic researchers, all with an employment background in industry, the study compared the production methods of the Japanese car manufacturers led by Toyota which were experimenting with Just-in-Time (JIT) production concepts and the mass production methods used by Western automotive companies.

The team, funded by a $5 million grant raised by a consortium of 36 car companies, each of which was allowed to contribute no more than 5 per cent of the total funding, looked closely at 90 automobile assembly plants in 15 countries. They found that in 1989 it took, on average, more than twice as many man hours to produce a car in a European-owned plant in Western Europe than in a Japanese-owned plant in Japan. Womack's people also found that Japanese-owned plants in North America took 25 per cent longer to produce a car, and American-owned plants in North America took 50 per cent longer, than Japanese plants in Japan; and that cars manufactured in European-owned plants in Europe in 1989 had, on average, 50 per cent more defects, as reported by owners, in the first three months of use, than cars produced in Japan.

'Lean production' was the term Womack's team coined for the production methods used by Japanese automotive companies. There were four main characteristics:

- eliminating all unnecessary production processes

- aligning all steps in each process into a continuous flow
- realigning workers into cross-functional teams dedicated to a specific process
- continually striving for improvement.

The main outcome is that fewer employees are needed to get the same number of cars to customers. Lean production methods also involve concepts that are now universally understood by manufacturers if not always universally applied. Because there may, literally, be only a few assembly minutes worth of components in the plant there cannot be any defects in these components since a defective one will stop production. This means that both assembly workers inside the plant and suppliers from outside it must share a total quality approach. Instead of inviting hundreds of suppliers to compete against each other to obtain short term contracts with the assembler, lean production requires assemblers to work closely with a small number of suppliers, inviting them to work as an integral part of the production development team.

There is no doubt that lean production methods, as outlined by *The Machine That Changed the World*, have revolutionised the automotive industry. Among the many Western companies that have benefited from lean production techniques are Chrysler, BMW, Volvo and Ford. In the UK, the most well publicised example of lean production, in Womack's sense of the word, is Rover. In 1987, Rover launched a Total Quality Improvement Programme, based on good communications and teamwork, preventing problems occurring rather than solving them after the event, managers ensuring that workers have the right tools and training for the job, and employees understanding that everyone has customers, whether inside or outside the company.

However, until 1991 the new team structure, based on 'cells' each consisting of two teams of 40–50 employees reporting to a team leader, was constrained by an outdated agreement with the unions. In September of that year Rover management proposed a new deal which granted workers single-status terms and conditions, job security and integrated manual/staff grading structure. In return for these benefits, workers agreed to the removal of all restrictions on overtime working, total flexibility in job functions and a devolved system of authority which placed maximum responsibility on the employee actually doing the job. In stark contrast with the past, teams at Rover are now responsible for quality, routine maintenance and housekeeping, involvement in plant/office layout and equipment, process improvements, cost reduction, control of tools and materials, work allocation, job rotation and training each other.

This level of devolution, which depends on a high level of commitment from the workforce, is supported by dedicated personnel practices such as rigorous selection processes lasting several days, single-status terms and conditions, and streamlined collective bargaining arrangements – including single-table bargaining, single-union deals, company councils or non-unionism.

Thus far, then, 'leanness' is easy to define. The problems start once you step outside the narrowly confined world of the car industry. As Christian Berggren, a Swedish expert in work organisation, argued in 1993:

> The sweeping assertions of Womack, Jones and Roos are based on their belief that car manufacturing still is the premier industry just as it was in the early 1960s; and that methods that promote productivity in the auto industry will of necessity do the same in other sectors. This view is certainly open to discussion. What, for example, do capital-intensive sectors like the petrochemical or paper making industries, or research-intensive sectors like pharmaceuticals, have to learn from the almost obsessive focus on hours per unit produced, so evident in the *Machine* book?
>
> Berggren (1993)

Berggren does not consider the problems of adapting Womack's philosophy to non-manufacturing sectors but it becomes very clear that the further you move away from car production the more hazy leanness becomes as a coherent philosophy. Throughout the early 1990s many organisations introduced new working practices that are capable of being termed 'lean'; but they also incorporate other business concepts and philosophies that sit next to, but are not necessarily synonymous with, leanness. These include:

- downsizing
- delayering
- decentralisation

- business process re-engineering
- kaizen
- total quality management
- knowledge management
- empowerment
- organisational learning.

How can we make head or tail of which of these concepts denote leanness in the sense Womack originally intended? In these circumstances, how can we predict with any accuracy the likely role of the HR function in either 'coping with' or 'building on' the changes brought about by a lean business strategy?

In our view, the intentions of the company in introducing leanness is the determining factor. Looking at the experiences of the organisations where we conducted interviews and those that have been written up in other recent personnel publications, three common reasons for introducing lean ways of working stand out:

- leanness to cut costs
- leanness to promote efficiency
- leanness to support growth and innovation.

It is useful to consider these options in turn alongside the four linked Figures 1–4. Organisations are attracted to pursuing leanness for three main reasons (Figure 1), which often reflect the relative power of the main stakeholders (Figure 2). Their underlying aim will certainly affect the choice of management concepts and measures adopted (Figure 3). It will also strongly influence the kinds of role the HR function is required to take on (Figure 4).

Leanness to cut costs

In these circumstances, downsizing becomes an end itself – and recent evidence from North America suggests that, in many industries, this is evolving from an act of desperation to a calculated

Figure 1 *What prompts leanness?*

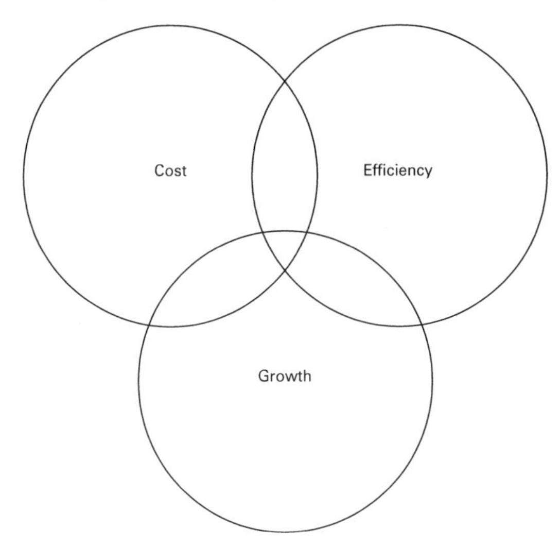

Source: Syrett and Lammiman, 1997

Figure 2 *Dominant stakeholders*

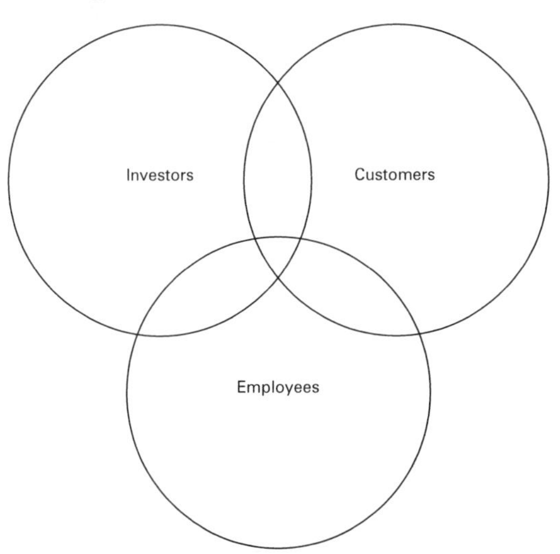

Source: Syrett and Lammiman, 1997

choice. The first downsizers were ailing companies; many of them had no choice but to go in for repeated bloodlettings as their businesses shrank and morale collapsed. But more recently a new sort of company has taken up the practice: successful firms that use job cutting to stay healthy in a boom market.

In the US, General Electric led the way, removing 104,000 of its 402,000 workers in 1980–90 even though it faced no great crisis. Others have started to do the same. Compaq cut its workforce by 10 per cent in 1992, despite healthy returns, because it thought the computer industry was bound to stay intensely competitive. Goldman Sachs cut its workforce by 10 per cent – not once but twice – to increase productivity. Proctor & Gamble sent away 13,000 workers even though it was the best performing company in its business sector.

In these circumstances – and it is a role older HR practitioners will be very familiar with – one of the personnel function's roles remains that of the 'kindly executioner' (see Figure 4). The familiar cocktail of voluntary redundancy schemes, redundancy counselling, early retirement packages and generous severance pay is still around but in the companies that practise this new form of downsizing – which presupposes that old style full-time jobs will be successively replaced by contract and outsourced ones – two newer measures have been added.

The first is an increased tendency for companies to choose who they want removed rather than let employees decide for themselves. Initially the methods have been very crude: last in-first out (which means companies lose all their bright young people); or the removal of everybody below a certain level in the hierarchy (which means that top heavy firms become even more top heavy); or the weeding out of all middle managers (which, as we will see later on, means companies lose a wealth of experience and connections through the loss of their corporate memory).

Now US firms are using more subtle means. The key, according to Karen Stevenson of UCLA's Anderson School, is to look beneath the corporate hierarchy and to find the informal networks that shape the day-to-day life of the company. The key figures in these networks, the people who shape the conversation in the corridors, are then used to

Figure 3 *Management concepts and practices*

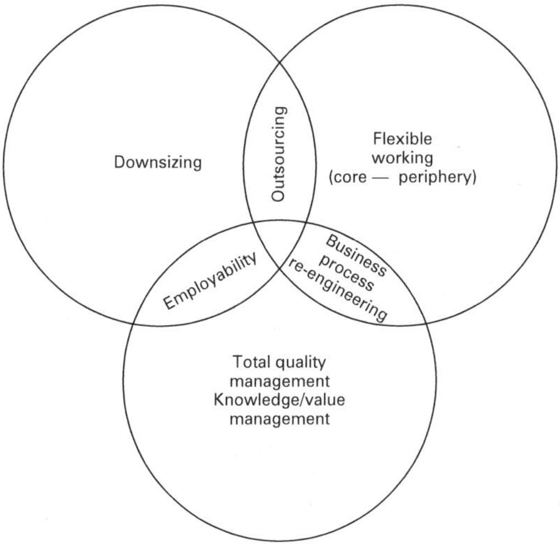

Downsizing
Outsourcing
Flexible
working
(core — periphery)
Employability
Business
process
re-engineering
Total quality
management
Knowledge/value
management

Source: Syrett and Lammiman, 1997

Figure 4 *The role of HR*

Kindly
executioners
Paymasters of
mercenaries
Systems
administrators
Corporate
physiologists

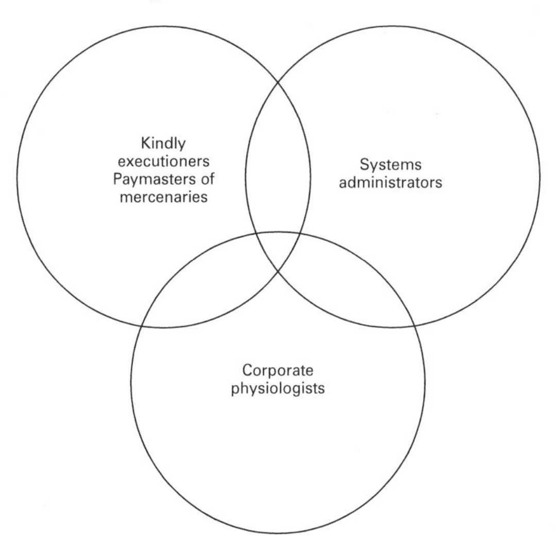

Source: Syrett and Lammiman, 1997

spread the bad news and are marked out as the ones to keep. The technique has been used a lot by US firms, including most notably IBM, but has yet to be imported in the UK.

The other new concept – employability – has been around on this side of the Atlantic for at least five years. The contract in this case, as *The Economist* recently put it, is:

> If workers promise not to make too much fuss when they are asked to leave, the employers promise to give them the opportunities they need to keep their skills up to date. For life-time employment read – one hopes – life-time employability.

The basic premise behind this 'contract' is not a bad one. Few people of any age believe in the concept of a life-time job any more but among the generation of young people now entering college or university lingering assumptions of job security simply do not exist. Surveys of student opinion suggest that young people now seem to take it for granted that they will have lots of different employers and perhaps lots of different careers during their working lives.

The difficulty with the whole philosophy of downsizing to cut costs, which the concept of employability symbolises, is that it creates two by-products that are potentially very damaging to companies – regardless of whether you take kaizen and quality very seriously. The first is a chronic absence of loyalty among key professional and managerial workers who can easily find work elsewhere, at a time when the links between employee loyalty, customer loyalty and return on investment are becoming more evident (see page 35). In these circumstances, a further role for the HR practitioner is the 'paymaster of mercenaries' (see Figure 4) in a land dominated by pay scales and where 'the going rate' is ruler.

The second is poor personnel practice and, ultimately, a collapse of morale in the HR function – who after all wants to be reduced to carrot and stick measures as the arbiter of effective personnel practice? The most vivid illustration of this is in the City of London, where over 250,000 people are employed in banks, insurance companies, and financial and professional services. With the exception of some (but not all) of the clearing banks, the City is the UK's best example of cost-based leanness. Following a temporary increase in staff numbers after 'Big Bang', massive restructuring and downsizing has led to around 150,000 jobs being lost in the UK financial services sector, most of them in the Square Mile.

One of the consequences has been a failure in personnel and training policies that has been identified as a factor in a number of major scandals including the collapse of Barings and the scandal at Deutsche Morgan Grenfell that was itself the precursor to the Nicola Horlick crisis described in more detail on page 36.

The failure of the HR function in the City was examined in detail by Roy Lecky-Thompson, former personnel director at the Bank of England, in a study published in *People Management* early in 1997 (Lecky-Thompson, 1997). The study was based on interviews with a cross section of line and personnel directors. As Lecky-Thompson commented:

> The feedback went beyond the usual whinging about the difficulties that HR experienced with senior line managers. There appeared to be a fundamental gulf between line and personnel expectations, which was seriously affecting personnel delivery.

Line managers and directors interviewed by Lecky-Thompson were uncertain about the role of personnel professionals and what they expected of them other than day-to-day administration. When chief executives wanted strategic input on people issues, they did not necessarily see personnel as the obvious choice. Personnel managers and directors were equally unclear about their strategic role, and the increasing pressure of dealing with difficult staff cases gave them little time to consider other issues.

Equally concerning, external commentators in the study felt that the profession's role in administering corporate downsizing had tarnished its image, while HR consultants commented that they now dealt directly with operational directors, bypassing personnel completely. Overall, Lecky-Thompson concludes, there is a real danger that the City's long-term competitiveness could suffer because excellence through people is practised by only a few organisations. 'If this happens,' he asks, 'will personnel remain on the margins, or will it be heading for extinction?'

Maybe, but not necessarily so. The significant and surprising turnaround of Lloyd's Corporation – examined in detail on page 69 – was achieved through an HR-led initiative that is a model of good personnel practice. The Lloyds experience shows that there is nothing inherently mercenary about the City and that the potential scope for people-centred strategies is as great at the hard edge of financial services as it is in less dramatically pressured industries.

Leanness to promote efficiency

Organisations that use leanness to promote efficiency draw on a number of traditions. On the bottom level is the 1990s version of the core–periphery model of the 1980s where a core of firm-specific staff is supplemented by an army of temporary and part-time staff, providing the numerical flexibility the company needs to deal with fluctuating economic circumstances.

In the 1990s version, however, greater emphasis is placed on outsourcing and contracting out services. These not only include basic services such as catering, cleaning, building maintenance, security and transport but also strategic services and functions such as accounting and – dare we say it? – personnel.

At a higher level, there is business process re-engineering. The emphasis here is more on Just-in-Time rather than kaizen. The quicker manufacture or speedier delivery of existing products or services, rather than the creation of new and better ones, is the main emphasis of most BPR initiatives. 'Doing more with less' is the most commonly used phrase.

In both cases the emphasis in this second type of lean organisation is on *how* people work; and the role of the HR practitioner is, accordingly, that of systems designer and administrator. As we will explore more systematically in Chapter 2, the new forms of working most commonly associated with lean efficiency – teamworking, outsourcing, professional part-time working – require new management systems and skills.

In a 'less means more' ethic, increases in performance have a high priority and some of the most important work HR practitioners have undertaken in recent years has been to design new performance measurement and appraisal systems that will work effectively in organisations based on teamwork and project management. Equally the management skills involved in coordinating the work of contract workers, agencies undertaking outsourced work and part-timers require a shift away from direct supervision and towards facilitation and support. Substantial work has been undertaken by HR practitioners in designing new competency frameworks that define and clarify these roles.

In all this activity, however, the HR practitioners' response to the drive towards leanness for efficiency has been reactive. Research by the Centre for European Human Resource Management at Cranfield School of Management (Brewster *et al.*, 1990) suggests that even if there is an HR practitioner on the board, organisations pursuing drives for efficiency rarely consult the personnel function when developing corporate strategy; most commonly, the HR director is presented with the corporate plan as a *fait accompli* and asked to develop a personnel strategy to support it.

Leanness to support growth and innovation

The first two types of lean organisation are united by one factor: they are cost-driven – the first explicitly, the second implicitly. The motivation driving the first is that organisations will only survive, even in times of economic stability and prosperity, by constantly stripping out excess fat. It also presupposes that the dominant factor tying workers to the company is financial – the current going rate and the maintenance of the individual's value in the job market through the acquisition of more skills and greater work experience.

The motivation driving the second is more subtle. It is driven more explicitly by market needs but the implicit underpinning is still one of cost-cutting. Our ability to serve the customer more effectively – by keeping prices low, delivering faster, responding more efficiently – can only be maintained if we manage our resources effectively; and 'managing our resources effectively' means delivery of the maximum productivity from the minimum resources. Leanness, in both these cases, has become an end in itself.

The flaw in both these arguments is they equate productivity with time and value with process. As we will argue throughout this book, being lean should not be the goal organisations strive for; rather they should aim to be fit. Certainly they should avoid being overweight, but once the optimum weight has been achieved, they should work hard to turn their fat into muscle, *where it is needed.*

In the 1990s, this means helping key employees to work smarter, not just harder. A growing proportion of tasks in the workplace require individuals to use their discretion and creativity. Empowerment has been defined by many consultants as the ability of employees to challenge or reinterpret tasks given to them by the organisation for the organisation's own good.

The third category of organisation, therefore, does not focus only on how people work but also on how they behave while they are undertaking the task. At the lower end of this scale employers will attempt to instil a kaizen culture – an ethic of continuous improvement of the type that has been advocated by 'quality' gurus like Deming and Juran for decades. Organisations of this type will combine process redesign with a culture change exercise designed to break down barriers between functions, provide staff with recognition, encourage employees to see staff from other departments as 'internal clients' and enable responsibility to be devolved to those workers closest to the customer. This change in culture will be supported by measurement and appraisal systems enabling the organisation to track increases or decreases in customer satisfaction, standards of service or product quality, and levels of employee motivation and productivity.

At the higher end of the scale, organisations will combine these traditional total quality management (TQM) measures with the proactive design of processes and the instillation of a culture that encourage a free flow of information and ideas, a tolerance of the unorthodox and experimental failure and an ethic of stakeholder management that links investor, customer and employee loyalty.

The dynamics of cost, efficiency and growth are best seen as concentric circles (see Figure 1) – they are not mutually exclusive.

Many of the US companies that have been voluntarily downsizing to keep costs low have also experimented with BPR, TQM and knowledge management. As we will see in Chapter 5, companies that have achieved renown for their TQM practices, like Kent County Council and British Airways, are facing economic forces that are obliging them to outsource operations and cut jobs.

Most organisations move from one circle to another as circumstances dictate and usually to a part of the diagram where the circles overlap. The majority started the journey cutting costs as a means to build a foundation for growth. But, as we will see later, the process is by no means a 'stairway to heaven' and unforecastable events will probably ensure that they all hover around in the middle for most of the time.

Three examples of fit companies

Rank Xerox

Rank Xerox has been a committed disciple of BPR since the early 1990s. Under the latest redesign of what the company terms its 'business architecture', where the efforts of the company are based around six core processes (see Figure 5), the various cycles involved in delivering effective service – buying, orders, delivery, billing, document creation, supplies replenishment and the maintenance and upgrading of machines – are visualised from the point of view of the customer.

The company goes to extraordinary lengths to identify the points at which the cycle might break down or fail to provide value to the customer. Under its recent initiative The Perfect Call, for example, customers' requests for their machines to be serviced or repaired are guided by a process that cuts down the need for on-site diagnosis and thus reduces response time, while at the same time maintaining a high level of service. Responses to calls occur within seconds, and much of the diagnosis is conducted over the phone, ensuring that the engineer arrives with an accurate picture of the problem and the right spare parts.

Figure 5
Xerox business architecture

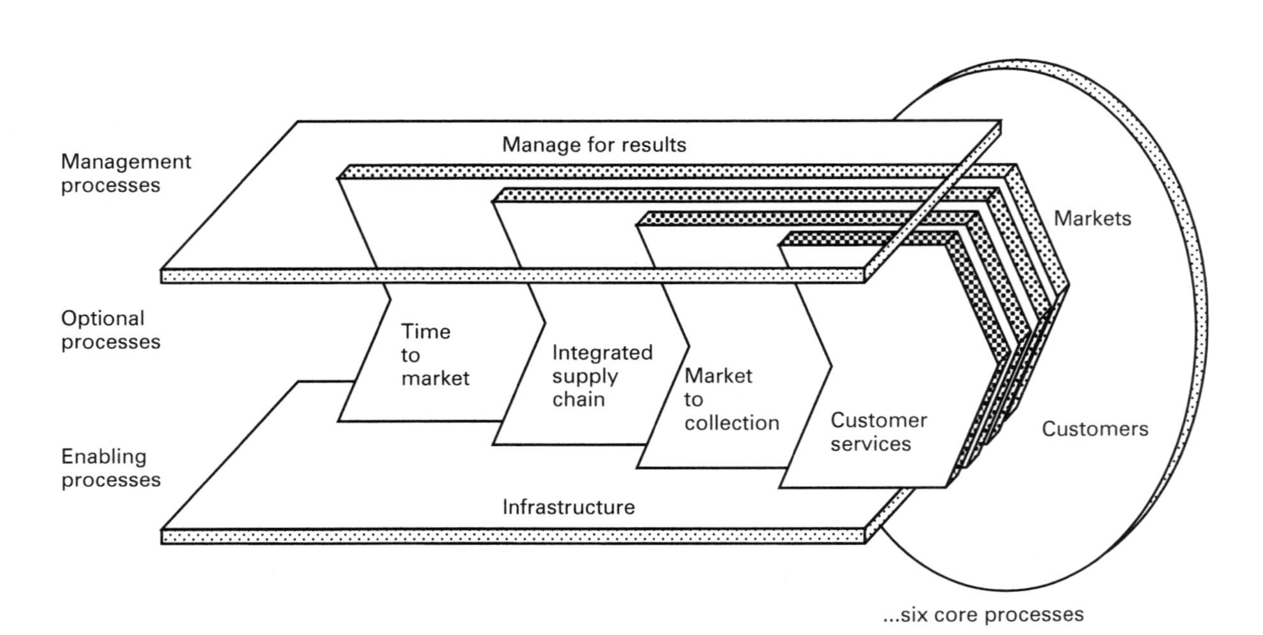

Progress in each of the company's key business objectives is continuously monitored against rigorous quantitative measures. Considerable effort is made to ensure that the measures used provide the right feedback. Measurement of customer satisfaction, for example, is assessed against the impact it has on customers' buying habits, not their opinions in a market survey. Olaf Odlind, Director of Marketing and MTC for Rank Xerox, sees this as an important measure that has kept the initiative on track: 'We recognise and create markets by spotting and pinpointing accurately emerging patterns of customer requirements.'

Rank Xerox's architecture is, like many TQM initiatives, market-led. However, in the redesign of its business processes, the key objectives of employee satisfaction, customer satisfaction, return on assets and delivering shareholder value form a virtuous circle (see Figure 6), reinforcing each other rather than competing for first place. In the last five years, for example, Xerox's return on assets rose from 6 to 19 per cent, alongside corresponding increases in customer loyalty and employee satisfaction. As Odlind says:

> We did not allow there to be any trade off in achieving these aims, so we would not, for example, allow any measures that boost productivity at the expense of employee morale because this would in turn undermine the quality of our customer service. Similarly we measure the success of our human resource strategy directly to our ability to achieve the right return on assets.

BMW

The use of BPR in promoting a free flow of ideas and information profoundly influenced BMW, Germany's leading luxury car manufacturer, when it invested over one billion Deutchmarks in a new R&D facility, close to the company's corporate headquarters in Munich, at the start of the decade.

The new centre, built on a 64-acre greenfield site acquired from the US Airforce, was the major plank in BMW's strategy to reduce the gap between the time it takes Japanese automotive companies to

Figure 6
The virtuous circle

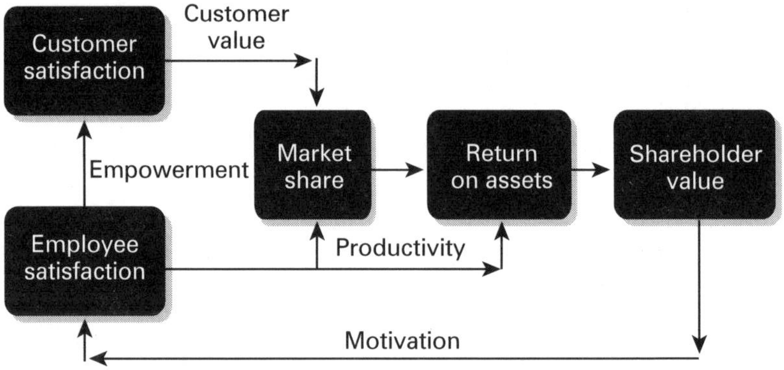

Source: Rank Xerox

design and produce new ranges of cars from scratch and that taken by its own R&D departments. Until the centre was launched in 1990, BMW's research and development staff were located in 12 different sites around Munich and the poor communications this generated were seen as a strategic albatross around BMW's neck.

Dr Wolfgang Reitzle, the creator of the new centre, called FIZ (*Forschung Ingenieur Zentrum*) was influenced by a piece of research by Boston's Massachusetts Institute of Technology in the late 1980s which suggested that 8 out of 10 ideas which led to breakthrough products or services were triggered by routine or chance encounters, for example over a cup of coffee. 'The effective flow of materials has long been understood as the governing factor in designing manufacturing,' he said at the time of the plant's launch. 'In like manner, we have adopted "the flow of ideas" as our design criterion.'

Accordingly, three governing principles lay behind the creation of FIZ:

- *Streamlining traditional hierarchies.* BMW's strategy called for all the functions contributing to the development of new models, and those which supply them, to be brought physically together.

These comprise research, development, technical planning, production engineering, quality assurance, value analysis and cost controlling, purchasing, logistics, patents and personnel. The layout of the entire complex and the occupation of each building is governed by the sequence followed in the design and development of new cars and not, as in the past, considerations of organisation hierarchy.

- *Imaginative allocation of space.* A detailed analysis of how new models are developed was carried out to discover which members of staff communicate with each other most frequently. As a result, development design departments are located adjacent to the corresponding production planning departments. The design engineer responsible for car doors, for example, works next door to the technical planner who will translate his work into a prototype model.

  All design offices are housed on the same floor as their model workshop, to ensure that staff from each communicate with each other by the shortest possible route. This means, for example, that a designer with an idea for a novel type of engine bulkhead can stop for a minute or two, wander down the corridor and find out directly from the robotics researchers whether a robot capable of the contortions needed to install such a design is available or capable of being developed. In this way, design engineers are able to follow the entire process of a vehicle's construction more closely, from design model to pilot series, and to study the results of their designs at first hand whenever they choose.
- *Appropriate building design.* The layout of the buildings that collectively make up FIZ are designed to support this kind of interdisciplinary collaboration. The site consists of a central workshop linked by covered overhead walkways to a series of satellite five-storey offices. Imaginative use of open-plan working areas, with few permanent structural walls, means that project teams can be created precisely according to requirements, without the need for structural modifications or the upheaval, dirt and noise caused by building work. The complex also incorporates a fully-fitted car assembly line capable of producing more than 3,000 cars a year. As Hans Honig, manager of welding and joining systems explains:

> This acts as a live 'testing ground', enabling designers to check how and in what conditions the parts they have designed are fitted on the assembly line, hand in hand with members of staff who are being trained to oversee the future production of the new series. Because production methods and procedures are tested in realistic conditions, problems can be identified and dealt with at an early stage, so that the start of production in other plants is much smoother.

Six years on, the plant has more than justified the time and financial resources BMW invested in building it. The highly popular 3-series model was designed and developed at FIZ. An innovative gas-charged lighting system and new welding and joining techniques are now being used on all models. Thanks to methods pioneered at FIZ, the company is also already making recyclable cars. Designers at the centre are now concentrating on making BMW cars 'greener' and safer.

Most importantly the development time taken by BMW to develop new models has been halved. Dr Bernard Pischedtrieder, the company's chairman and former director of manufacturing, argues that the design and manufacturing methods used at FIZ will reduce by a full two years the development time of a new series from blueprint to full production – giving the company a critical competitive edge in a country where labour costs are far higher than elsewhere in the world.

Oticon

The Danish company Oticon's turnaround at the start of the decade provides a further illustration of how corporate streamlining, if handled sensitively, can foster innovation rather than stunted growth. This time, however, an experiment at the company's headquarters was spread throughout the whole organisation.

The number one worldwide manufacturer of 'behind-the-ear' hearing aids in the 1970s, the company's market share began declining in 1979 as people started using 'in the ear' aids. By 1987 market share had dropped from 15 to 7 per cent and the company was starting to lose money.

A new chief executive, Lars Kolind, was brought in to transform Oticon's fortunes. At first he introduced a classic cost-cutting approach to leanness: decreasing costs, increasing market focus and cutting staff. In the short term these produced the desired results. By 1989, Oticon was making a profit and had begun to regain market share. Yet Kolind was aware that this was not enough; as he said:

> It was clear that we would not survive over the next five years without taking a radical step. Where was our competitive edge? Nowhere. We realised a possibility lay in designing an organisation that integrated all the capabilities for creating a superb hearing aid: digitalisation, micro-mechanics, audiology, psychology, sociology and sales.

Accordingly he launched the 300 Project, so called because its goal was to increase productivity at the company's headquarters by 300 per cent over three years. The main aim of the project was to trigger a breakthrough in creativity and innovation. Like BMW, part of the process involved a breakdown in traditional job and organisational structures. Jobs are now redefined around the individual. The company has also moved from a traditional hierarchy to what Kolind describes as a 'spaghetti' organisation in which project groups, consisting of multi-skilled workers, are reconfigured constantly with the changing workload.

However Kolind realised that this kind of business process re-engineering would not, in itself, provide the kind of breakthrough in innovation that the company needed. The way in which information and communications was managed required the same uprooting. As Kolind said:

> We knew that there was a lot of knowledge out there that was not being used. So we changed all communications from memos and formal meetings to information conversations or dialogue. We got rid of nearly all paper by using an imaging computer system and scanning all incoming mail before shredding it in the paper room. However we also discouraged the alienation process that often occurs with computerised management information systems by discouraging e-mail and encouraging people to talk directly with each other.

The changes are not confined to Oticon's headquarters. Using lessons learned from the 300 Project, Kolind has organised production in manufacturing plants in 30 countries into departments of 30 to 50 which, in turn, are divided into product families with working groups of eight or nine people.

Each member of the group learns all the operations of each of the other members of the group, and then the operations of all other groups. As a result, everyone is cross-trained and can work in any other group. Once again, training in group communications is central to the process. Workers are encouraged to come up with ideas on how to improve their work. They then implement the solutions themselves after having involved those people who would be most impacted by the change.

These measures finally provided Kolind with the productivity increases he was looking for. In the first two years of the project, there was a 15 per cent increase in efficiency. Re-work time dropped by 37 per cent and material costs by over 70 per cent.

The methods pioneered by Kolind in the early 1990s also played a large role in helping the company to produce a string of new products including most recently DigiFocus, the first fully digital compact hearing instrument, which won the 1997 European Design Prize. Oticon also won the European IT Award in November 1996 for its groundbreaking internal management system.

Conclusions

It is evident that in all the three examples above leanness is an important part of the organisation. Many of the features of Womack's concept of lean production – eliminating unnecessary processes, aligning processes into a continuous flow and so on – are still an integral part of the production and service cycle. The easy transfer of ideas, resources and skills to where they are most needed would not be possible if the 'fat' hierarchical structures, and the lazy ways of working which went with it, still clogged up the company's arteries.

However excessive dieting is not enough. As Womack himself stresses (1996):

> Because lean methods are much more efficient, fewer employees are needed to get the same number of products to customers. Management has two fundamental choices at this point: lay off workers or find new work by speeding up product development and finding new markets. The second choice is clearly the correct one because otherwise management is asking employees to cooperate in the task of eliminating their livelihoods.

In all these organisations, leanness is not an end in itself but a stage towards becoming fit, rebuilding the muscle – a motivated workforce supported by the right resources – that provides the organisation with the energy to compete in its chosen activities. Oticon's Lars Kolind commented after he decreased costs and cut staff in the late 1980s: 'Where was our competitive edge? Nowhere . . . we knew that there was a lot of knowledge out there that was not being used and we wanted to tap it.'

2

Aspects of Leanness in Context

In Chapter 1, we covered a lot of ground very quickly. It becomes very clear from looking at 'lean' organisations that as a direct result of becoming lean they have introduced new working arrangements that, while they are not synonymous with leanness, are a direct by-product.

The purpose of this chapter is to look at some of these concepts and practices in more detail and highlight some of the practical issues raised by their successful implementation.

Teamworking

Teamworking and effective project management are at the centre of the lean organisation. Almost all successful UK employers have moved in some respect from a functional framework, with line managers responsible for specific functions within the organisation, to a matrix structure with core firm-specific roles such as product development, the installation of new systems and the introduction of quality processes undertaken by cross-functional teams. The case studies of BMW on page 15 and Oticon on page 18 demonstrate the indisputable commercial advantages of this aspect of delayering.

However, the organisational implications of this transformation, particularly in terms of the additional burdens and skill requirements it places on key managers and technical and professional staff, is very great indeed and often very subtle. Teams, in essence, become a microcosm of the organisation. Even with the right balance of creatives, resource gatherers, company workers, completer-finishers and chairs or leaders in place, as advocated by Meredith Belbin (Belbin, 1996), if the right level of teambuilding and a culture of cross-company collaboration is not in place there will still be a tendency for people to fight for their own patch and withhold key information.

Moreover, at a time when the link between innovation and lean ways of working is assuming a greater importance, it is worth stressing that not everybody works well in teams and there is a tendency for teams collectively, under intense financial and time pressures, to stifle or inhibit individual initiative or activity. Research by Marsha Sinetar of MIT in the 1980s (Sinetar, 1985), for example, shows that while creative thinkers, the 'plants' in Belbin's model of team roles, are not always wild-eyed nonconformists and in most of the small customs of life may be ordinary and even boring people, their ability to add value to the organisation's activities thrives on freedom in three important areas of their working life:

- freedom in the general area of their work and the way in which work gets done
- freedom to ask novel or disturbing questions
- freedom to come up with unusual solutions to the things they are thinking about – sometimes in the form of what seems, to others, to be wildly impractical ideas.

In the context of a tightly run team working under pressure, these freedoms are often in short supply. Creative thinkers wind up alienating other team members by focusing on pet projects and their own idiosyncracies; they often feel isolated and misunderstood, 'a loner'; they can be perceived as self-serving, disruptive to team effort and a frequent breaker of rules and protocols; and, if these symptoms are unchecked or badly dealt with, they can suffer from feelings of loneliness, depression and stress.

The increasing diversity of team members – with different nationalities, educational backgrounds and functional expertise – also means that they will have different sets of success criteria. Design engineers, for example, are primarily interested in creating the best possible design to achieve a perceived objective; they are concerned about the production process, but this tends to be of secondary relevance. Production managers, on the other hand, concentrate fully on the production process; they are less interested in the effect of the most efficient process on the organisation's cash flow or marketing performance. In the computing field, software engineers have different objectives or success criteria from hardware specialists.

Project leadership

All of this places a huge responsibility on the individual leading the team. The project leader not only has to coordinate the work of the 'visible' team, who have a direct input into the project and who probably meet collectively on a regular basis to manage the project, but also that of an 'invisible' team made up of those who may not have a direct managerial role but whose views are vital to the success of the project. Clients and end-users of the product, outcome or innovation the team is producing are the obvious ones; less obvious are those who will be affected by the project in some way or another and who need to be kept informed of progress.

In an era of stakeholder management (see Chapter 6), recognising and reconciling the interests of everyone who has a stake in the project is often a highly delicate process. In one recent case, a manager working for a computer systems company was asked to take over a prestige project to introduce a computerised typesetting and layout facility for a major national newspaper. The project was already in mid-cycle and the client had demanded the replacement of the existing project team because client managers were not being kept fully in touch with progress. In these circumstances the project leader had to contend with:

- the expectations of senior management within his own organisation – who regarded the project as vital to the company's reputation
- the needs of senior management within the client organisation – who were dissatisfied with progress and felt excluded from the planning process
- the demands of technical staff within the client organisation – who had specific requirements of the system being introduced which were not being met
- the problem of assembling a new team which, for political reasons, needed to include some members of its demotivated predecessor
- the difficulties of keeping this team in touch with each other when its members included both American and European advisers
- the delicate exercise of negotiating additional financial resources when the project was already badly over budget.

Because of the nature of projects and their management, project leaders need characteristics not necessarily required in line or functional posts. While it is obviously useful to have the appropriate technical background, a project leader needs to have an understanding of the politics of the organisation to help the process of identifying and assessing the project's key stakeholders; the necessary skills to exercise financial control; and finally considerable people-management skills, not only to lead the team but also to obtain the necessary financial or technical resources from, for example, a recalcitrant functional head of department over which he or she has no direct control – a task requiring considerable political adeptness and negotiating ability.

Self-directed teams

If anything, the latest manifestation of lean organisations – self-directed teams (SDWTs) consisting of groups of employees who have day-to-day responsibility for managing themselves and the whole work process – imposes even greater demands on the effective running of the organisation.

In theory, instead of taking direction from supervisors or a nominated project leader, these teams take direction from the requirements of the work itself – the production schedule, orders received, customer demands, etc. SDWTs are therefore 'work centred'. Typically they plan, schedule and organise production or service delivery, monitor performance and improve work processes.

In more advanced stages of development they choose team leaders, select and train new team members and participate in performance evaluations and discipline – administrative and strategic support activities traditionally undertaken by senior line management or HR departments.

The organisational implication of supporting this transformation is immense. In addition to ensuring that, individually and collectively, team members have access to the right information and skills in decision making, the move to self-directed team activity requires a fundamental re-think of the role of middle managers – something we shall explore in greater depth below – and the right organisational support systems.

Budget, financial and operations performance monitoring systems need to be modified to support SDWTs. Reports which, in the past, went to supervisors or middle managers, need to be redirected. Information needs to be reorganised so as to capture team responsibility for a whole product or service.

HR systems may need major readjustment to ensure that they are aligned with the transfer of decision making and the restructuring of work. Recruitment and selection procedures must reflect the need of team members. Job evaluation and the redesign of working practices need to reflect the increased delegation of authority and decision making.

Empowerment

The trend towards self-directed teams forms part of the larger movement towards greater empowerment at lower levels of the organisation. As we saw in Chapter 1, restructured companies and a greater emphasis on philosophies of quality and continuous improvement have led to flatter career structures with more responsibility being placed in the hands of front-line staff.

The theory of empowerment is attractive. Staff are nearer to the customer and therefore better able to challenge existing procedures and systems on their own initiative. Because they have greater discretion in their work, they are more fulfilled. Ten years ago, Charles Handy likened the process to a doughnut. The jam in the middle of the doughnut is the essential elements of the job, its core functions. The dough represents the greater discretion in how staff fulfil these core activities.

However, the consequences of this greater freedom are often negative rather than positive. In 1994 Roffey Park Management Institute undertook a survey of over 200 firms to examine the career implications of flatter career structures (Holbeche, 1994 and 1995). Although

Table 1 *Effects of delayering on individual employees*

	'Yes' responses (%)
More responsibility	72.4
Less responsibility	5.5
Bigger span of control	44.5
Smaller span of control	5.5
More teamwork	49.0
Less teamwork	8.2
More autonomy	43.8
Less autonomy	12.3

Source: Roffey Park Management Institute, 1994

Table 2 *Effects of delayering on staff as a whole*

	'Yes' responses (%)
Morale up	12.4
Morale down	65.5
More work to do	72.4
Fewer promotion prospects	78.6
Increased teamwork	49.7
More staff leaving	25.5
Better retention	4.1

Source: Roffey Park Management Institute, 1994

managers in the companies surveyed acknowledged that they had more responsibility, more autonomy and more opportunities for teamwork (see Table 1), this was felt by many to be threatening rather than fulfilling. Morale in these organisations had fallen, flatter structures meant that there were fewer opportunities for promotion and there was greater staff wastage in key areas (see Table 2).

The comments published in the report reflected these concerns. People felt they were 'expected to do more with less', suffered from 'increased workload' and 'far more work with less support', believed that there was 'less time for people development', 'responsibilities were less clearly defined and therefore led to increased stress', and that people generally were 'expected to work effectively in areas for which they were not trained or that they had no experience in'.

Two particular concerns were raised in the report. The first was that in the process of delayering, whole swathes of administrative staff had been culled out of the organisations surveyed with the result that professional staff were badly supported and felt they were being asked to reach targets without the appropriate resources to do so. Secondly, many managers in the survey found the level of discretion given to them threatening because the extent to which they were able to operate on their own initiative and the boundaries of good and bad practice were not being spelt out consistently and clearly by the organisation. There was, in particular, a discrepancy in what constituted right and wrong use of initiative between different departments. In these circumstances managers tended to play safe and be highly risk averse, confining themselves to the 'jam' in the doughnut and therefore fostering a culture exactly opposite to that the company had intended and planned for.

Outsourcing

One of the most significant recent by-products of the lean organisation has been the strategic use of outsourcing on a scale never envisaged by commentators in the 1980s. Outsourcing is the most tangible manifestation of the 'core–periphery' model of manpower planning identified by John Atkinson of the (then) Institute of Manpower Studies in 1984 (Atkinson, 1984) and Charles Handy in his theories about the shamrock organisation outlined in his book *The Future of Work* (Handy, 1985).

Using the shamrock or core–periphery model, organisations divide themselves into the two types of employee. The first is a small professional 'core' of employees who undertake functions highly specific to the firm and which are guaranteed job security in return for a willingness to be constantly retrained or redeployed. This group is supplemented by a mass of part-time, temporary short-term contract and casual workers, allowing the organisation the numerical flexibility to increase and decrease their workforce in line with its economic performance and circumstances, and, significantly, the wholesale contracting out of functions and departments that are not central to the organisation's 'core competencies' – the process now called outsourcing.

In the late 1980s the process was confined largely to ancillary functions like catering, transport and cleaning. In the early 1990s the process has been extended to functions which would previously have been seen as central to the company, such as accounting, IT and customer service, and which therefore involve professional, technical and managerial staff who would previously have been categorised as 'core' under the shamrock philosophy.

In 1991, for example, BP Exploration (BPX) broke new ground in the oil industry by outsourcing its accounting function and staff, plus the associated accounting software and IT support groups. This was not a one-off decision but part of its long-term strategic focus on core activitities.

The decision affected the entire accounting operations services of the company's UK Continental Shelf operations. It was taken against the background of maturing oil fields and the rising costs for BPX in mining the North Sea. Since 1980, production costs had tripled, while in real terms the selling price had slumped to a third of what it had been. To remain profitable, BPX had to reduce its spending substantially and it is now on target to achieve annual savings of up to 30 per cent.

To decide which functions to retain in-house and which to contract out, the company divided its accountancy function into the following categories:

- accountancy policy (based on professional judgement)
- interpretation of financial information
- production of financial and management information
- processing of input transactions
- software support for accounting systems
- provision and maintenance of computer hardware.

The first two functions were considered core and required an internal knowledge that would be hard for any supplier to acquire, unless they had a detailed knowledge of the oil industry. The remaining functions (which represented 90 per cent of the accounting function) were deemed to be capable of being handled just as easily from the outside. Accordingly, more than 300 BPX staff from six locations were transferred to a single site in Aberdeen run by a chosen supplier, Andersen Consulting. The operation, Accounting Services Aberdeen, now handles all BPX's accounting functions, while BPX retains control over developing policy and interpreting and using the information to manage its business.

Nor is this process confined to the private sector. At about the same time BPX outsourced its accountancy functions, Berkshire County Council contracted out its entire range of financial services including those that would previously have been seen as core functions, such as the provision of technical and corporate financial advice, as well as more routine services such as payroll, pensions and creditor payments. Tony Allen, Berkshire's chief executive, recently commented:

> I see great merit in having a much smaller, cohesive local government, concentrating on its strategic activities, accounting to its public more effectively and not being distracted by employing tens of thousands of staff. If you have a bureaucratic, monolithic type of organisation, outsourcing is one way of slimming it down and getting a grip of the core business.

There is no doubt that outsourcing brings significant benefits to the lean organisation. In addition to cost savings and service improvements in the case of BPX's outsourcing exercise with Andersen Consulting, for example, more prompt payment of suppliers has enabled supplier partnering arrangements and discounts to be optimised. Single point control of cash management has also reduced funding charges by £500,000 a year.

However, there are also fundamental management and HR considerations in adopting this strategic kind of outsourcing. An arm's length arrangement might provide an illusion of comfort but, precisely because the level of investment in dedicated systems and approaches is that much greater, the effects of the arrangement breaking down may be similarly great and may have severe consequences. In effect, the organisation's reputation is on the line regardless of whether the function is handled in-house or out of house.

In practical terms, therefore, there needs to be a clear definition of boundaries. Complex service agreements will only work in practice if the organisation undertaking the exercise has given careful thought to which functions should be retained in-house and which are to be outsourced.

In addition, there need to be integrated points of control. These should be supported by legal agreements, social ties and shared values. The BPX contract, for example, is managed by a joint review board of three representatives of each company. The responsibility of this board is not only to review the relationship between the account manager working for the supplier and the key manager from the customer acting as the interface, but to exchange information about each other's business and review the long-term development of the project.

More significantly, the strategic outsourcing of key functions that would previously have been regarded as 'core' is likely to have important and sometimes destructive affects on the morale of the workforce. In the first place, the transfer (or re-employment) of staff to the consultancy or contractor undertaking the job may raise difficult issues. British Airways, for example, outsourced its baggage handling and check-in functions as part of a strategic attempt to cut its cost base by £1 billion in the light of calculations that, because of the falling revenue per passenger affecting all airlines, they would no longer be in profit by the year 2000. The transfer not only raised real concerns among the staff being transferred about their pension rights, but also about the reduced lack of pride and fulfilment they would experience in no longer working for a company with a blue-chip reputation. How British Airways dealt with these issues is explored in greater depth on page 55.

Secondly the message outsourcing on this scale sends to the workforce that remains inside the core of the organisation is 'no one is safe'. The essence of the deal for 'core' workers under the principles outlined by John Atkinson and Charles Handy was that provided core staff were prepared to be constantly retrained and redeployed *within the firm* their job security was guaranteed. Strategic outsourcing of the type undertaken in the 1990s shows that there is no rigid definition of which functions in the organisation are 'core' and which are 'peripheral'. If the staff in an accounting department interpreting financial information can be outsourced today, for example, who is to say that the staff determining accounting policy will not be outsourced tomorrow?

Flexible working

The widespread use of the core–periphery model has worrying implications for other members of the 'periphery'. The last 15 years have seen part-time and temporary work rise as a direct result of this aspect of leanness. Less than 50 per cent of the labour force in the European Community are now permanently employed full-timers (IPD, 1994). Part-time working is on the increase in most countries with Germany, the Netherlands and the UK leading the pack. Formal fixed-term working is more prevalent in some countries, particularly in France and Germany where legislation encourages its use; in others, such as the UK and Sweden, temporary and more casual forms of working account for most of the increase.

In a sense, then, this kind of work is no longer 'peripheral'. Many professional and managerial workers with 'core' skills (ie skills that would previously have been seen as essential to the firm) have chosen, or are being forced, to work on a self-employed, freelance or part-time basis. These include not only working mothers who are unable to work full-time because of family commitments but a growing army of professional and managerial workers of both sexes who have been outsourced or placed on short-term contracts by the dramatic restructuring of organisations that the lean revolution has provoked.

But whatever the exact nature of the working arrangement and the type of worker involved, one effect unites them. They are all moving outside the ambit where employers feel any responsibility for their careers or long-term professional development.

For a privileged few, flexibility has provided the opportunity to win lucrative contract and consultancy work, which will provide a far better income than exercising the same skills in a full-time job. For the majority, it has meant a reduction in job security and – critically

– the loss of their ability to keep their professional skills up to date.

The long-term dangers of this combination of circumstances were illustrated vividly in a report published by the Institute for Employment Studies at the start of the decade (Varlaam *et al.*, 1989) which examined the training needs of the broadcasting industry in an age when the BBC and major ITV companies no longer train more technicians, journalists and production staff than meet their immediate manpower requirements.

The survey stressed the gap that was growing between the training received by broadcasting employees and that received by freelancers in an industry where over 40 per cent of skilled technicians and professional staff are freelance. It found that 39 per cent of broadcasting employees had received some form of training in the previous 12 months compared with only 11 per cent of freelancers. Television journalists received particularly poor levels of training. Around 33 per cent had received no initial training in any type of journalism, 75 per cent had received no specific training and only 16 per cent had received formal training in the previous 12 months.

The report highlighted concern among both large broadcasters and small independent production companies that, at a time when satellite and cable television was currently coming on stream, the skills of half the industry's workforce would be progressively degraded. As a direct result of the report, new training standards were agreed which could be applied by training consortia responsible for developing the skills of independent workers.

The learning organisation

The dangers inherent in having up to 50 per cent of the UK's workforce experiencing a successive degradation of their skills have a direct bearing on another concept that has been partially provoked by lean ways of working – the learning organisation.

Thinking about the learning organisation has undergone substantial revision as more organisations try to put the concept into practice. Considerable progress has been made in finding new ways to develop the individual. Thanks to the efforts of leading companies and business schools a new set of tools, techniques and resources now complement or replace classroom-based programmes. It is less clear whether this admirable activity is actually benefiting the organisation. Most HR practitioners have accepted, as an act of faith, that developing their employees using these techniques will, in itself, enable their business to adapt and respond more readily to constant change. Among the many consultants and academics who parrot 'learning pays' on conference platforms, there is also a tendency to assume that *creating* the talent organisations need is the same as *tapping* it.

Hard experience has shown that this is not the case. The rise in interest in organisational learning in the late 1980s went hand in hand with the creation of systems, cultures and practices which could have been tailor-made to undermine any benefit the organisation might gain from the concept. These are still in place in many UK organisations and include:

- inappropriate performance measures, based on narrow output targets, rather than processes which involve staff more closely in achieving corporate goals
- the poor use of internal labour markets, so that only a small proportion of employees are appraised and developed systematically
- flawed communications systems, which place too much emphasis on computerised data and electronic interaction and not enough on the creative serendipity which results from routine social contact between workers engaged in key tasks.

The glaring omission has been a failure to understand the context in which effective learning and innovation takes place.

Organisations need to tap talent that is increasingly expressed in intangibles such as emotions, energy, creativity and know-how. Yet many still use task-oriented and instrumental ways of organising their workforce and create pressured working atmospheres, fuelled by insecurity, long working hours and cost-driven targets which undermine their contribution to the organisation's collective capacity to learn.

Managers and professional staff adjust to the added pressures and work harder, but sooner or later something has to give and it is usually the very qualities that the company needs most – their alertness and commitment.

As Anne-Marie Garden of the Harbridge Consulting Group commented recently:

> Individuals want to make full use of their talents in what they do. If this is not achieved in an organisational setting, other outlets are found at home, at leisure or in smaller organisations which have re-invented the rules for working arrangements and lifestyles.

Employability and the growing issue of loyalty

Let's review for a second the implications of some of the trends that we have explored in this chapter. As a direct result of lean ways of working and the widespread use of core–periphery working, flexible workers now make up anything between a quarter and a third of most organisations' workforce. With the current fashion for re-evaluating core competencies and outsourcing any function at any level which is not competitively critical, this proportion is likely to increase. Yet flexible workers are among the least motivated, developed and valued members of the labour force. They are typically excluded from the social fabric and culture of the organisation. Their progress is often not linked to any formal career appraisal scheme and they are frequently excluded from company training provisions and the opportunities for promotion.

At the same time, core workers are being placed under intolerable pressure. Working long hours to achieve high standards, frequently without the necessary administrative support, they often lack the intellectual space and constructive environment to deploy 'right brain' thinking and make the maximum use of their insight and creativity. The organisation's capacity to learn from their knowledge is therefore impaired.

Equally damaging has been the failure of organisations to replace a job-for-life commitment with any tangible response that recognises employees have career interests which stretch beyond the needs of their immediate job.

The fashionable concept of 'employability' – which assumes that employees consciously accept less job security in return for opportunities to develop new skills and expertise which then stand them in good stead after the current job – has been undermined because most employers fail to live up to the rhetoric.

In industries where there is a high percentage of knowledge workers, such as banking and financial services, this can have lethal consequences. A report published four years ago by a consortium of City-based employers, including blue-chip companies like Coopers & Lybrand, NatWest, Slaughter and May, and Royal Insurance, found that perceptions of staff about the exact nature of the 'employability deal' have undermined trust in employers (Rajan, 1994).

The report, which highlighted increases in turnover of nearly 50 per cent among City-based staff in the early 1990s, concluded:

> Current efforts by employers to promote employability and empowerment are perceived by middle managers and staff as a one-sided deal . . . Those sensing better opportunities elsewhere are going in the belief that the 'grass is greener on the other side'.

Indeed the report found that 40 to 65 per cent of staff would consider changing their jobs if they had the opportunity.

As the City markets moved from bear to bull in the mid-1990s, the predictions made in the report have proved all too prophetic. By the start of 1997 private investigators, including the famous Kroll Associates, were being called in by leading investment banks in the City to alert them to likely defections among key staff. Telephone conversations at work and even social chatter in public places were being secretly tapped; meetings in conference rooms were being bugged; and the contents of computer hard disks were being examined for evidence of disloyalty.

This extraordinary spate of activity, more reminiscent of spy thrillers than the financial pages, came on the heels of a highly publicised showdown between Deutsche Morgan Grenfell and the top-performing head of its £18 billion British pension fund operations, Nicola Horlick, who was suspended after allegations that she had tried to persuade 20 colleagues to follow her to another bank.

The Nicola Horlick brouhaha, now lodged in the distant memory of most people, is worth recalling for a number of reasons that have a direct bearing on the business implications of lean ways of working:

- *In the lean organisation, front-line staff* are *the business.* They provide the value added. In the light of the Nicola Horlick crisis, Morgan Grenfell was forced to engage in a damage limitation exercise to reassure its clients about the loyalty of its remaining fund managers.
- *In a situation where leanness becomes meanness, and traditional values are replaced by a dog-eat-dog culture, loyalty among junior staff often transfers from the employer to the individual manager.* Nicola Horlick was suspended, not because she considered a job offer from a rival firm but because she was allegedly trying to persuade other colleagues to join her. In the media scramble that followed, many of her staff and colleagues remained doggedly loyal to her, to the detriment of the company's reputation. It transpired that confidence in senior management had been undermined by a management purge that had followed a scandal in DGM's unit trust business the previous year.
- *The reputation of the company counts.* Companies cannot afford to trade on old reputations that have been undermined by restructuring, downsizing and redundancies. Two centuries of tradition at Morgan Grenfell amounts to very little these days because, after Big Bang, the takeover by Deutsche Bank and numerous internal scandals, the firm is no more than another aggressive and soulless trading house in the eyes of its staff. As we shall see in the case of Birse Construction on page 48, there are plenty of means at DGM's disposal to stop the rot – all of which the company has so far failed to adopt.

It is, of course, very easy for businesses outside the City to scoff and comfort themselves that DGM, and firms like them, are merely getting what was coming to them. However, after five years of downsizing, outsourcing and cost cutting, few industries can take the loyalty of their staff for granted.

In a follow up to their 1994 survey, Roffey Park Management Institute (Holbeche, 1997) found that half of the professional and managerial staff they re-interviewed in 1996 were likely to look for another job in the light of the perceived career prospects (or rather the lack of them) with their present employer. A fifth were hoping for a new job within the following year and a third expected to move within one or two years.

Among the other facts to emerge from the survey, perhaps the most significant is that greater numbers of senior managers than middle managers were actively looking for another post. In some cases this was because they felt more vulnerable and exposed; in others it was because they found their idealism about the company had changed substantially for the worse as they were exposed to the factors that really influenced key decisions – a significant number of these being directly connected to the more negative aspects of lean ways of working.

Anecdotal evidence from people interviewed in the survey shows the high price companies pay when loyalty breaks down – and also the unintentional negative consequences of what happens when delayering is poorly implemented. In one organisation a computer department was outsourced to an outside contractor which followed common practice by re-employing many former staff. The internal staff responsible for managing the contract lacked the technical knowledge to spot the fact that major computer fraud was taking place. The scam was eventually exposed by one of the former employees but not before the company had lost thousands of pounds What is perhaps most significant, however, is that many former employees had chosen to remain silent.

Conclusion

The purpose of this chapter is not, in any sense, to argue that organisations should return to the working practices of the 1960s or 1970s, or to throw doubt on the strategic advantages of lean ways of working – as we saw in Chapter 1, these are immense.

However, the potential of 'the lean organisation' is often being undermined by short-sighted employment practices and a failure to understand the human implications of transformation on this scale. These are all problems which can be rectified by measures that fall directly within the ambit of the HR function. In Chapter 3 we shall look at how a number of organisations have coped successfully with the human implications of leanness and in Chapter 4 we shall draw some conclusions on the strategic role HR practitioners can play in the process.

3

Fitness in Practice

In the last chapter we looked at the potential pitfalls of lean ways of working at a time when the social and economic conditions that existed when it was first introduced have changed. In this chapter we will look at how organisations from very different backgrounds have adapted to these changing conditions – moving from a few of the general characteristics they share to the specifics of their individual situations.

Consultations with customers and stakeholders in the front line

As we argue throughout this book, leanness is not an end in itself. Among the best firms, it is nearly always triggered by a quality or continuous improvement initiative designed to devolve responsibility to the front line in order better to meet the needs of customers and other key stakeholders in the communities where the organisation is active.

Involving stakeholders in the change process, for example through surveys, focus groups and meetings, is also important because the priorities the restructuring process is designed to meet may not be as clear-cut in the customer's or recipient's mind as they are in the minds of senior managers.

The Kowloon and Canton Railway Corporation in Hong Kong, for example, has been undergoing a quality and continuous improvement process since the early 1990s which has involved extensive restructuring of its core services (Syrett, 1995). Central to the process has been a series of initiatives designed to canvass KCRC customers about the changes the company has been making. These include customer service centres, which attracted 60,000 comments and enquiries in the first three years of the process, passenger forums and passenger liaison groups.

From the feedback they received KCRC found that with a million passengers travelling on a stretch of track only 34 kilometres long (the distance between Kowloon and the old Chinese border), few people expected comfortable or adequate seating in the carriages. They placed a far higher premium on punctuality, reliability and efficient ticketing. The feedback changed the emphasis of the early BPR process. Let us look now at an example nearer to home.

Kent County Council

Kent County Council has been undergoing a major restructuring programme since the mid-1980s – a process initiated by the authority's present Chief Executive, Paul Sabin, appointed in 1985.

Paul established three basic management principles which lie at the heart of most effective 'lean' strategies:

- *Closeness to the customer* – ensuring that the focus of attention is on the sharp end of the organisation, where staff have everyday contacts with customers.
- *Devolution* – giving managers the decision-making power necessary to do the job. This means that they control the resources necessary to provide their services effectively. Individual responsibility and accountability becomes much clearer. Managers with devolved budgets and decision-making authority, KCC argues, can overcome bureaucratic processes which previously prevented decisions being made in the best interests of the service being delivered.
- *Management not administration* – expecting managers to be accountable within a clear corporate framework for the management and performance of their part of the organisation, rather than solely for processing and controlling activity over which they previously had no influence.

Of the three principles, the second – the devolution of budgets – has had the most impact on the organisation. As Mike Dudding, head of corporate review in the corporate resources department, one of the architects of the reforms, explained:

> These front-line managers had never had a budget before. We

> went very quickly from having a single budget for each primary service to many hundreds of individual budgets, each with an individual budget manager. It took some time to work. Initial enthusiasm for freedom to get on with the job turned to recognition they were accountable for their actions. Managers needed resource support alongside them. So, along with devolving budgets are devolved accountancy support to each budget holder, people who were very suspicious of what they initially saw as interlopers coming into their patch. The first signs we saw that things were working was when the 'devolved' accountants, previously seen as part of the centre's control mechanism, started to fight alongside the social services and education managers for more resources. Managers started to challenge traditional thinking, take risks and push out their boundaries. There was a lot of innovation going on.

This innovation has been increasingly important as the 1990s have progressed and the budget restrictions imposed on local authorities by central government have become greater. Staff at Kent have become accustomed to having to deal with increased demands on reducing budgets while working hard to bring about service improvements and to raise standards. Some of the more important changes that have occurred since the devolution of budgets first occurred have included year-on-year budget reductions that have forced efficiency savings and reduced non-core activities; and the introduction of competition in the provision of some aspects of services, together with an internal market with support services operating to nil budgets.

All of this has required a great deal of flexibility in work practices among groups and individuals. Staff have often needed to work beyond their original professional groupings, as they have taken on new responsibilities demanding new skills such as budget management and performance improvement. Individual members of staff have increasingly been involved in project groups, task forces and pilot groups trying out new approaches to solving problems.

Kent has also introduced a strong ethic of local democracy, sustainability and priority of service provision to those in need. As a result, irrespective of the service that staff have been involved in delivering – whether assessing the needs of an elderly person living alone at home, those of a young child with severe physical or mental disabilities, or meeting the needs of the public for information on new subjects – staff are used to working on two levels. The first involves performing the required task – arranging a care package, or linking up with other professionals involved with care, or retrieving relevant information in response to enquiries from library users. The second involves also thinking strategically about the long-term demand for the service. There have been major national reports and commissions about key county services over the past few years, and education, social services and the arts and libraries – as complex services facing increased public expectations – have been particularly influenced by the national scene. There has been unprecedented change in these services. However, in turn managers in the front line have been able to influence the national committees: partly because Kent, as one of the country's largest authorities, is listened to and partly because managers have been proactive in the piloting of new ideas.

It was against this background that in 1995 the education department initiated a review of the process by which children with special educational needs are statemented – ie the development of a formal 'statement' that confirms they need dedicated or specialist care and identifies appropriate action. The statement binds the various agencies to give the support. At the same time the process involved in getting a child statemented was slow, sometimes taking two years or more. Mike Dudding, the manager responsible for conducting the review, determined that a formal BPR process might speed this up.

Dudding's first action was to consult external experts.

> I had been researching BPR techniques and how they were used. I went to talk to staff at King's College Hospital in London where the Government had backed an exercise done by them together with a firm of consultants that had undertaken this kind of exercise before. One of the things that had impressed me was the approach they had used in consulting key stakeholders likely to be on the receiving end of the newly structured service *before* they came up with a design, so that everyone could gain a proper understanding of what the issues were and the energy and commitment the process had created with the hospital staff. As a result we decided to consult widely in the early stages of the exercise and I undertook to provide some corporate funding to support this.

With the support of an expert from the Strategic Planning Society, the KCC project team ran a series of one-day sessions open either to those directly affected by the service or involved – teachers, educational psychologists, education welfare officers, speech therapists, health workers, paediatricians, parents and the education department's professional staff.

> We mapped our understanding of the process of statementing on enormous sheets of paper on a wall and then asked participants to comment on it. We handed out 'Post-its' and then invited them all to scribble down what they thought of the process – whether we had understood it right, where it was strong or weak and where the key trouble points were. These were wonderful sessions. We attracted hundreds of comments. Not only did it give us a new perspective of how key stakeholders regarded our service, it created dialogue between groups of professionals and consumers that we had never achieved before.

A steering group was set up to pool the comments gathered from the workshops and translate these into a workable process. To help members of the group do this, the project team came up with the novel idea of each member 'role playing' a key stakeholder in the process. One played the child, another the parent, a third the social worker and so on. The group played out the process, informed by the feedback they had received from the workshops, and the results highlighted vividly where the existing system was breaking down. As Dudding says:

> The parent was shut out. Nine times out of ten, the parent, who knows the child best, is not informed about what is going on, is not consulted at any time and is denied a voice in influencing the care strategy. It was the one thing we had overlooked in our early planning.

Equipped with this new insight, a further series of workshops were arranged to develop alternative models for the process, once again involving all those who had a stake, including parents. Some of the issues that emerged included the fact that it was always the most articulate parents that got the quicker result, that few professional workers came up with 'whole family' solutions and that there was no guarantee that the school would follow through. What parents wanted was greater advocacy for the child, a mechanism to ensure that the statement is enacted, support for parents in the form of counselling and a helpline, and training in special needs for teachers, caseworkers and classroom assistants.

A series of 10 radically different models for delivering the service emerged and the steering group selected three of them to examine in detail. Pilot schemes have now been set up and the initial feedback is very favourable. An example of the assessment model is provided in Figure 7.

A key factor in the exercise was the positive reaction the consultation process provoked in KCC's professional staff. At the start of the exercise in September 1995, in a prophetic statement, one of the principal assessments officers commented:

> It will be interesting to receive the feedback from the forthcoming workshops being attended by parents, the major stakeholders in the process. I am confident that a positive action plan will emerge from this initiative, and all those involved, including parents, will benefit from sharing their frustrations and concerns, and their highs and lows. Something must be learned from this alone and it can only improve the way we do our jobs.

Dudding himself is delighted that this prediction has been fulfilled, and he concludes:

> It was a real buzz for me. I was amazed by the commitment of parents and the time they were prepared to put into the exercise. It may seem an expensive process in terms of time or money, given the number of people involved. But as a result of the effort we put into it, we realized that we hadn't understood the problem. We thought it was about speed of processing. In fact it was about lack of consultation and involvement of parents.

Revitalising the workforce

Early moves towards lean ways of working will almost certainly have a detrimental impact on the morale and loyalty of the workforce. If the process has involved substantial job cuts or outsourcing, then the 'survivors' will feel pain at seeing friends and former colleagues losing their jobs, guilt at the fact they have survived and, in an organisation reduced in size, will face the prospect of working with added workloads, related stress and poorer conditions.

Figure 7

SEN three level assessment model
Pre-school SEN process and the three routes
to LEA-funded support

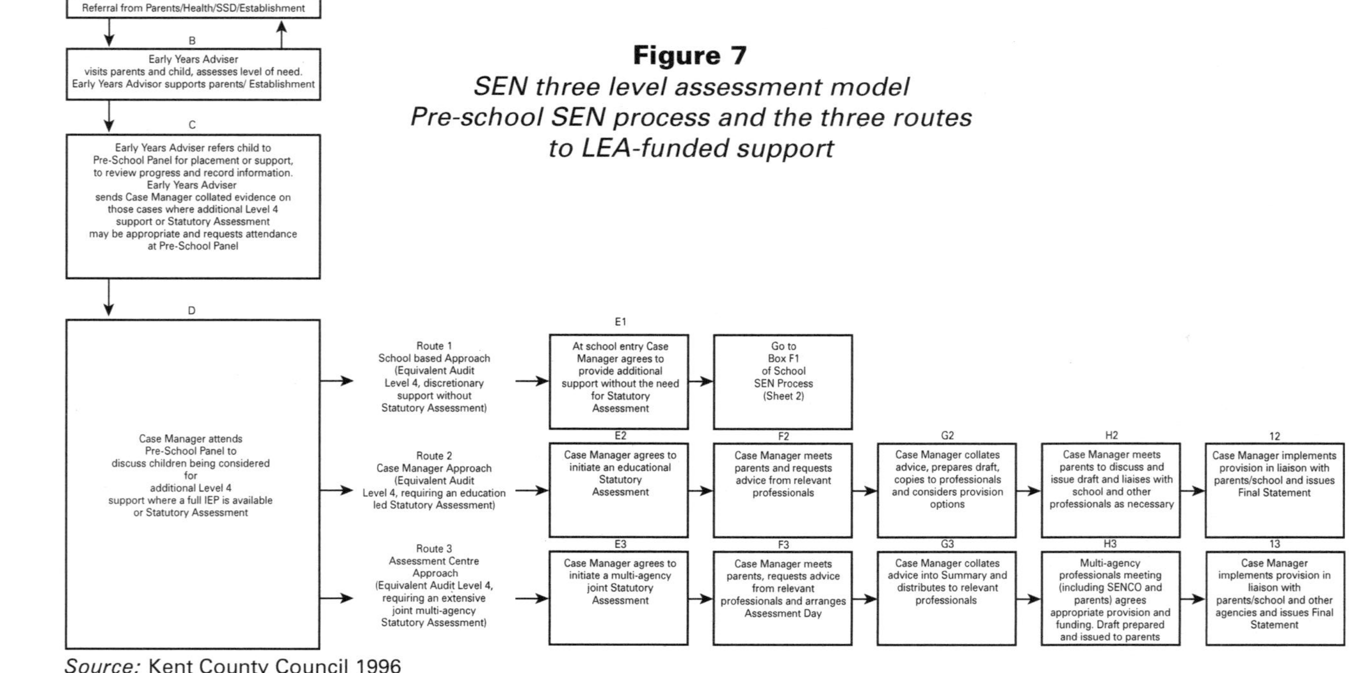

Source: Kent County Council 1996

Sometimes the trauma of the job cuts is so great that the memory buries itself into the folklore of the organisation for years afterwards. In one site previously owned by ICL and now by Zeneca, managers continued to refer to Black Friday when 50 per cent of the staff was laid off, and continued to take cautious low-key decisions in order to play safe despite the fact that the lay-offs had occurred 10 years before.

Yet even if the restructuring process involves little or no enforced redundancies, the potential impact on the organisation can be every bit as great. Left unchecked, the workforce will often lose a clear sense of direction. They may be unsure if there is any real corporate vision or whether it is all a knee-jerk reaction. They may not understand the new vision or may prefer the old one.

Communication, or a chronic lack of it, is nearly always at the heart of the problem. It is not just what is said but when it is said, how its is said and how often. What is not said may also be important. One of the most dysfunctional facts, when change is being introduced, is long silences coupled with irregular and poor communication. These tend to stimulate rumours and contribute to the tendency for staff to play safe wherever possible.

Some of the more important measures to counter this potential problem include:

- *Communicate consistent messages about the direction of the business*. People lose confidence in an organisation's future because they lose confidence in its management. The burden is on senior managers to reassure employees that they have a well-thought plan for the future and to communicate that plan clearly.
- *Communicate the 'why' and the 'how' of the change*. Employees need a clear understanding of the rationale for change, such as controlling costs and improving customer service. They also need to know how external forces are driving the need for change and how these forces affect business priorities.
- *Generate excitement about the future by painting a vivid picture of what the organisation intends to become*. Then develop and implement a local translation process to help each part of the organisation determine how it can participate. This process, together with *asking them what they think* brings strategic goals to life and

allows employees to 'own' the restructuring process and its results.

- *Identify and develop the right strategic skills.* Specific competencies will be needed for future success and they are likely to be different from those required in the past. Many companies identify these competencies by looking for employees who perform their jobs the way they should be done in the future. They then focus their HR processes, including recruitment, training and development, on developing the required capabilities.

Birse Construction Ltd

In 1994, Teesside-based Birse Construction embarked on an ambitious education programme to revitalise its entire workforce of 1,100 employees. Founded in 1970, Birse's early success had been built on principles of customer care, autonomy for managers at every level, and honest dealings with employees, subcontractors and suppliers.

Two developments in the early 1990s badly dented Birse's corporate values. Rapid expansion between 1990 and 1991, which took the company from a turnover of £115 million to £316 million, led to a rapid increase in the number of employees. Many of them, however, were recruited from other contractors more used to rough and ready ways of doing business. In addition, by the beginning of 1994, Birse was suffering from the aftermath of the recession. Profits were greatly reduced. It was evident that the company had lost sight of some of its original principles. Internal surveys of the workforce suggested that morale was low, communications and client perception were poor, staff turnover was high and no common culture existed between the various regions.

The strategy adopted by Birse was designed to restore confidence in the company's values. Using methods pioneered and supervised by the consultancy 5DM, 480 managers attended a series of two-day seminars and 620 employees attended one-day courses. These provided them with teamworking and project management skills and tuition in how to manage their careers more effectively. A new staff appraisal system and personal development plans were introduced, while surveys to monitor interdepartmental and client perception were stepped up. Refresher workshops were held at regular intervals as part of a maintenance programme. In the words of Steve French, the senior manager at Birse responsible for running the change initiative:

> A lot of our people had got the impression that they had to be something they weren't. They thought that we wanted them to be aggressive and even dishonest in the way they worked. The biggest message they have received from this initiative is that this is not the case.

As a result of the programme, staff turnover at Birse has dropped by 65 per cent since 1994, approval by clients has practically doubled and negotiated work is up by 45 per cent, as the company has won back clients previously alienated by the old aggressive culture.

Birse has also negotiated long-term partnerships with major customers, based on a quality approach to contracting that would have been impossible to deliver with a discontented workforce. According to French, the company's recent partnership with Rover is a direct result of the cultural transformation Birse has undergone in recent years – a transformation mirrored by Rover's own culture change programme.

French also argues that the emphasis the 5DM programmes place on life skills will underpin the company's commitment to sustainable business performance:

> If you think that the world is a great place then your actions will reflect this. If you think it is bad place then the way you act and speak will reflect this too. We are attempting to get people to think differently and come up with new solutions. This excellence, we hope, will not be undermined by changing economic circumstances.

Middle out: transforming the role of the middle manager

In revitalising the workforce the new role of middle managers is likely to be critical. The demise of middle managers as a direct result of lean ways of working has been exaggerated. A recent study by Incomes Data Services (IDS, 1995) found that although all companies IDS surveyed had made middle managers redundant as a result of delayering, only one said they had been disproportionately affected.

The experiences of another, Cornhill Insurance, illustrated that middle management redundancies are not an inevitable accompaniment of leanness. Cornhill's delayering started in the summer of 1994. It was part of a wider reorganisation aimed at improving efficiency and customer focus. Following complaints that it was taking far too long to process policies, the bureaucracy was streamlined and some branches were closed. At the same time, the number of management grades was reduced by two to four and job requirements were revised. However, Cornhill stressed in the survey that the aim of the changes was not to reduce middle manager numbers, but to increase efficiency. Out of 110 middle managers, only around eight or nine left, and this was mainly because those involved did not want to relocate. It is also worth stressing that two other organisations in the survey, Land Rover and Courtaulds, pointed out that it is often difficult to separate the changes faced by middle managers from either the impact of the recession or wider reorganisation.

However, the IDS survey also found that although middle managers have enjoyed little or no influence over whether or not delayering or empowerment takes place, they are usually in the front line when it comes to putting the policy into practice. Precisely because they have most to lose in any form of restructuring, because their jobs are often at stake, they frequently exhibit the least commitment to the process. The implications of this are all the more grave because, as HR functions have been delegated to line managers, the responsibility to respond to employee concerns over the planned changes now rests with the people who are least enthusiastic about the process. Putting it bluntly, if middle managers are not on board, they will not motivate employees and they may try to sabotage the change process – often successfully – by dragging their feet or speaking negatively about senior managers' decisions and priorities.

Organisations that have been most successful in overcoming this potential barrier have found ways of clarifying or transforming the role of the middle manager, thus providing incumbents with ownership of the process and an incentive to make it succeed. The measures have included:

- involving middle managers in the decision-making process at an early stage, particularly if the company is considering making job cuts or outsourcing decisions
- supporting middle managers in their efforts to manage the expectations of employees, for example by providing them with training in counselling and by producing literature and/or audiovisual materials
- re-evaluating the role of middle managers. Often this is best achieved by building on traditional management responsibilities but changing the emphasis. In managing performance and expectations, for example, there should be less assessing and more involvement. In resolving differences and conflict, managers should strive for consensus and avoid a direct exercise of their power. In managing processes, more attention needs to be paid to information management, and, in building an environment where learning is encouraged and supported, there should be less direct supervision.

This tranformation in behaviour is not always easy to achieve. Middle managers often feel their status rests heavily on their power to tell others what to do. This is especially true in large organisations with a long tradition of operating through specialist functions. Comfortable in a world of specific plans and actions, middle managers can find it acutely uncomfortable to ask themselves or their juniors to think through what their goals should be.

In this respect a well-designed competencies framework, which places more emphasis on behaviour rather than simply on technical ability, has been found by many organisations to be critical in helping existing managers to adapt their behaviour; such a framework can also provide a more effective set of criteria against which new candidates can be assessed. Investment in new criteria of this kind is all the more important because, as one senior manager put it, 'Middle managers have everything to fight for in the post-BPR age. The jobs they are most needed to fulfil are up for grabs.'

Rolls-Royce Motor Cars

For the better part of the 1990s, Rolls-Royce Motor Cars has been undergoing an unprecedented transformation of its manufacturing operations at its Crewe-based plant. The traumatic first phase, cutting its output and workforce by half, was forced on the company by the worldwide collapse of the market for premium cars during the 1990–91 recession.

The second phase, more in the tradition of 1980s-style TQM, involved transforming its production process into the team-based system favoured by so many of its mass-market rivals. Assembly workers have been transformed into 'associates' led by team leaders rather than foremen. A continuous improvement programme entitled 'Strive for Perfection' has been coupled with lunchtime forums, during which staff have the opportunity to quiz senior managers on matters of concern.

The move has been spearheaded by the massive reinvestment in new manufacturing technology involving an automated gantry-based assembly process unique to Rolls-Royce, which has cut assembly time by three-quarters, and the introduction of a new plant which enables the company, for the first time, to construct the bodywork of their cars themselves – a function previously undertaken on Rolls-Royce's behalf by a subsidiary of Rover Cars.

A further spur to the new culture is the highly personalised approach that the company uses to sell one of the world's premium products. Potential customers are actively encouraged to visit the Crewe plant and are shown around the plant by former or current site workers. The company estimates they will attract 3,000 visitors a year because of this recent initiative. The assembly teams are, therefore, in the public eye. Each division – ranging from upholstery, through woodwork, to metalwork etc – has created visual displays of their craft and individual members are often brought over to speak to visiting purchasers. The idea that you as a customer have spoken to the person who built your walnut burr dashboard or polished the radiator is used as a strong selling point. 'Built for me by someone I know and who knows me' is a common slogan used by the assembly teams.

The transformation has not been achieved without difficulty. The company had to work hard to overcome the old adversarial culture that was a legacy of the 1980s and the cutbacks of the early 1990s. Christine Gaskell, personnel director, is the first to admit that the company had an appalling record of communications with the work-force:

> Explaining the reasons behind the changes we have introduced and making sure that people understand what is in it for them is something the organisation tended to underestimate in the early years of the Strive For Perfection campaign. We have got much better at it but we are still learning.

The second related problem is the vacuum left by a gap in middle management. The cutbacks in 1991 left the company's middle management layers stripped to the bone and the subsequent quality campaign commenced from the bottom up, putting the team leaders first. In the words of Mike Flewitt, production director:

> What was left in place after 1990 was the absolute minimum management that could support the immediate requirements. The result was that until last year, despite all the efforts to introduce a team-based culture, it was crying out for leadership. There was great inconsistency in the way team leaders undertook their role. What managers we had had little experience of the new production methods we were using and were very constrained by what they had done in the past.

The decision was made to adapt the layer of first line managers into 14 'zone' managers to supervise the team leaders. Personnel manager Paul Victor explains:

> We made a conscious decision to keep the number of levels within the organisation as it was. However, in defining the roles of the zone managers we did not emulate companies like Toyota or Nissan where management roles are based on process time but rather based it on the number of people they were responsible for. The roles needed to be entirely appropriate to our organisational strategy and culture and could not, therefore, be simply transplanted.

The consequence of this decision is that the zone manager's behaviour was as important as his or her technical skills. It was on their shoulders that the task of turning what was left of the adversarial culture into a spirit of cooperation and innovation would fall.

To underpin the selection process, Christine Gaskell won the approval of the Board for a new competency framework that would ensure selection was undertaken consistently and fairly. The framework was developed by a benchmarking process that examined how other car manufacturers had restructured their businesses and by consultation with Roll-Royce's own workforce. Very importantly, the vacancies were thrown open to the team leaders as well as Rolls-Royce's existing managers and outsiders. Of the thirteen that have been appointed to date, six have been appointed from existing management positions: one is a sideways move from an engineering position, three are external appointees and three are former team leaders.

The fact that only three appointments have been external has sent important signals to the workforce, Gaskell believes:

> At the start people thought that this was a ruse to get rid of our existing management population and bring in 14 outsiders. The fact that we have promoted three team leaders surprised and delighted many people. However, even more importantly, it has validated the competency framework as the most consistent and fair way of recruiting. Many of the applicants we recruited had the right technical knowledge but could not apply it with the behaviour needed to foster the culture we want. Go back two years and they would have been recruited into the business.

As a result, she continues, the framework they have created is now being applied to other parts of the organisation:

> It is often difficult for a manufacturing organisation to make the move from being task-focused to adopting any management approach that smacks of touchy-feely. The fact that it is now accepted across the organisation is a testament to its consistency. We want to be like Blackpool rock. Cut us anywhere and you will find people believe they are getting consistent leadership and are no longer getting mixed messages about where we are going as a company.

Meeting the unions halfway

As we stressed in Chapter 1, the exact nature of leanness depends on the context in which it is introduced. This is particularly true when it comes to negotiating necessary agreements with trade unions, particularly in brownfield sites where there is generally a strong trade union organisation and existing agreements that impose relatively rigid demarcations between job functions.

Historically trade unions have been publicly hostile to lean production methods but privately pragmatic. The introduction of the majority of the initiatives most commonly associated with leanness – delayering, multi-skilling, cross-functional teamworking, core–periphery working, individual employment contracts – has taken place in the UK at a time when trade union membership has been in decline, union bargaining power has been diminished and a hostile government has imposed severe legislative restrictions on industrial action.

In addition, the most painful aspect of leanness – downsizing – has taken place during a recession which has affected blue and white collar job security with equal severity. Industrial action over delayering and business process re-engineering was limited during the early 1990s. However, there are now signs that this may be changing – and it is important to understand the reasons why.

The subtle shift in the IR agenda is best illustrated by the events which led up to the strike by British Airways cabin crew during the summer of 1997. The lead up to the dispute was attempts by BA management to come to terms with a financial paradox that was affecting their rivals as well as their own company.

The paradox – which, like all paradoxes, is not solvable but only capable of being adjusted to – is the equation between the cost of running an international airline versus the revenue it can expect to earn from each passenger. Throughout its recent history, BA's cost per passenger has consistently risen faster than the revenue that each individual passenger is willing to pay. This dilemma is not confined to BA in an industry where companies cannot afford to price themselves out of the market – and it is one of the reasons why airlines have lost more money than they have ever made in the history of aviation.

BA traditionally managed this anomaly through a combination of constantly increasing the number of seats in their aircraft and managing a better 'yield mix' – persuading people to trade up to a higher fare within a cabin or, better still, to trade up to a more expensive cabin. By the end of 1996, these options were disappearing. Aircraft were as full as they could be without the passenger systems in airports and on board breaking down completely. As a result, 40 per cent of the company's potential source of profits was gone and, with current trends, senior management calculated that the company would be losing money by the year 2000.

The only answer was to cut costs and the cuts that were needed to keep the company in profit were staggering – over £1 billion from the permanent cost base. The new policy was dressed up in fine language – The Business Efficiency Programme – but this did little to disguise the fact that 5,000 jobs needed to be cut and that non-essential services such as ticketing and catering would have to be outsourced.

To meet their aims, BA needed to persuade the unions to accept some hard mathematical truths. As one of the managers responsible for the negotiations commented:

> We went to the unions and put the problem to them. We are now in a position where, due to market forces beyond our control, we are spending too much. We have covered this overspend well over the last few years but now we are up against the stops. We are paying certain categories of staff as much as 30 per cent above the market rate – we need to fix it if we are to stay in business.

An internal survey carried out at the start of the consultations suggested that 90 per cent of BA's staff accepted the need for the cuts and by the beginning of 1997 BA's management had reason to hope that, while discontent rumbled beneath the surface, they had averted an all-out strike by any of the unions.

It was too much to ask for. The company was able to negotiate a settlement with their ground staff over the sale of its catering services and its pay proposals for cabin crew were accepted by a small breakaway union Cabin Crew 89. But 9,000 cabin crew members voted 2–1 in a secret ballot to strike in July 1997.

The Transport and General Workers Union (TGWU), the union

representing most of the striking workers, has a well-established history of pragmatism when negotiating over new working practices. It was responsible for the Rover deal (see page 2) which pioneered lean manufacturing methods in the UK and, early in 1997, the same year as the BA strike, signed a ground breaking deal with Blue Circle which involved acceptance of sweeping changes in working practices in return for staff status for workers and a degree of job security. Bob Ayling, BA's chief executive, has also pioneered a less macho culture at BA, publicly disapproved of the dirty tricks campaign against Virgin and has close links with the present Labour Government. So what went wrong?

Two reasons stand out:

- The deal between Rover and the TGWU struck a balance between the interests of the company and the union. On the one hand, the company's genuine need to become fully competitive was fulfilled. On the other, the independent trade union structure, albeit within a new joint trade union bargaining forum, required to represent the needs and aspirations of TGWU members was retained. The spirit of collaboration of the Rover deal was not present in the BA negotiations. The job cuts were imposed, and striking members were threatened with dismissal and legal action for damages. While this is entirely within the law, it did not create an atmosphere conducive to settlement.
- BA negotiated a series of commitments to its workforce during the 1980s, the two principle ones being: 'we will support our people and respect their needs and concerns' and 'we will be open and seek to involve our people as much as possible in achieving change'. Many BA staff feel that senior management pays only lip service to these commitments and that a gap has grown between senior management and the workforce. The Business Efficiency Programme has none of the hallmarks of earlier programmes like Putting People First in 1984 and Fit for Business in 1989, where top directors attended seminars and workshops to gain commitment from front-line workers face to face. In particular the negotiations over the job cuts took place at the same time that Ayling launched a new marketing campaign designed to position BA as a

> global airline. Unlike the campaign which immediately preceded the privatisation of the company in 1987 – spearheaded by the slogan 'The World's Favorite Airline' – where Sir Colin Marshall waited until commitment from staff was in place, little has been done to gain the workforce's commitment to the new campaign.

Senior management at BA respond by pointing out that while staff overall understood the reasons for the cuts, the employment relations equivalent of NIMBY is in operation – 'so long as it isn't in my department' – and that they have put in place a generous voluntary redundancy and retirement scheme with suitable retraining in areas where new skills are required. However, the strike has highlighted the fact that the quality-based reforms introduced by Lord King and Sir Colin Marshall – which were predicated on gaining commitment from the workforce – are running out of steam.

There are a number of important indicators arising from the BA experience. Relationships with unions are linked directly to the atmosphere in the workplace. Commitment from the workforce, however successfully won, will not last unless it is renewed and senior management remain true to the values that won this commitment in the first place.

Above all the workforce – and the unions which represent them – are usually only prepared to accept jobs cuts and changes in working practices so long as they can see corresponding benefits they bring to relationships in the workplace. The agreement negotiated with the unions at Rolls-Royce Motor Cars in 1991 took place at a time when recessionary conditions made it easy for management to impose a 50 per cent cut in the workforce. But the corresponding changes to working practices, from a top-down to a team-based culture, is lauded by many of the front-line workers as a major breakthrough in work-based relations. 'You no longer need to leave your brain at the factory gate,' said one team leader.

The necessity to bear these factors in mind is all the more important because the major unions, including the TGWU, are now pushing harder for agreements which exchange labour flexibility for a greater measure of medium- and long-term employment security. 'The fact is that both we and the unions would like to renegotiate the agreement we made five years ago,' says Rolls-Royce's Christine Gaskell. 'However, the stability it has brought to the workplace makes us feel that we do not want to open this can of worms.'

4

The HR Practitioner as Corporate Physiologist

The overwhelming conclusion we drew from researching the case-studies in this book is that organisations should not strive to be lean; they should strive to be *fit*.

Research by Professor John Stopford of the London Business School (Baden-Fuller and Stopford, 1993) suggests that much of the delayering that took place in the early 1990s actually had little to do with a calculated strategy to create greater efficiency or competitive edge but was little more than crude cost cutting during a severe recession dressed up as something more refined. Only after the effects of the cuts started to hit the bottom line did a quality-based approach to lean ways of working appear on the boardroom agenda. As Professor Stopford argues, many companies survived the recession of the early 1990s only to plummet or go under because their management processes are geared up to maximise the efficiency of their existing resources rather than to enable the organisation to win new business.

The issue is not, Professor Stopford stresses, a matter of small versus large or the well-resourced versus the impoverished. The companies that succeed, maturing beyond their first flush of success, are those whose capacity to innovate is built into their culture and management systems.

This is borne out by our own case research. Both Rolls-Royce and Rank Xerox, for instance, slashed their workforces radically in the early 1990s to survive the collapse in their markets. Almost immediately the negative effects of this 'delayering' decimated productivity and morale – as Christine Gaskell at Rolls-Royce comments:

> We had a situation where people were treading water; they were not in any way moving forward.

This is not to suggest that any of the organisations we interviewed wanted to return to being 'fat'. Rather they strive to find the right balance between carrying little or no excessive weight but at the same time building up resources where they are most needed. The dilemma was put rather prosaically by James Butcher, a learning adviser working for Kent County Council:

> There is a paradox in the design of organisms, which is how much of their finite resources to invest in the survival of the individual, and how much in increasing its chance of reproduction, and hence the survival of the DNA. . . . Maybe it is true of organisations as well. An organisation is like a gene: its members are the biological mechanism by which this gene reproduces itself in the future. If you slash R&D, the slack in the system to experiment etc, then you increase the chances of the current gene-carriers' short-term survival (keeping costs down and the organisation afloat), but only by risking the chances of passing the gene on. Conversely if you overinvest in R&D and costs get out of hand you risk making the current gene-carriers unviable, in turn risking the chances of passing the gene on.
>
> It isn't enough to strip out layers of management without reinventing what management means. Otherwise the same tasks and processes get shared out among fewer and fewer people. So we need a new language to live in a new land.

The new language, we argue, is the language of fitness, not leanness. To achieve this peak, and thus the creative culture needed to compete in a radically more competitive Olympic tournament, the corporate athlete needs the right medical advice and the right fitness regime – and this is the point at which the HR practitioner finds his or her new role.

If we see HR practitioners as a new breed of corporate physiologist, what sort of roles should they be playing to help corporations stay fit and build muscle – in terms of additional resources and ideas – where they need it? Just as paramedical responsibilities can be separated easily into groups of responsibilities, so do the main functions of the HR practitioner (see Table 3 on page 62). Let us look at the most important of these functions as they relate to the move from leanness to fitness.

Table 3 *Comparing the roles of physiologists and HR practitioners*

Physiologist	HR Practitioner
Diagnosing, sensing, observation	Assessing training needs, consulting, monitoring
Assessment, prognosis, treatment	Evaluation, long-term/ strategic planning
Blind trial, controlled trial	Pilot scheme
Counselling, applying balm	Counselling, employee support
Personal trainer, physio-therapist, lab technician	Skills trainer, mentor, training officer
Laying down muscle	Redeployment and cross-training

Source: Syrett and Lammiman, 1997

Diagnostic, sensing, observation

As devolution and empowerment has increasingly placed responsibility on the front line, the relationship between greater responsibility and higher pressure has pushed certain parts of the corporate body, weakened by excessive delayering, to the point where it can no longer bear the load being placed upon it.

Three causes stand out. The first is the lack of administrative support provided to professional staff, combined with over-extended spans of control, which have resulted in workloads well beyond the capacity of most individuals. The rise in stress among managerial and professional staff has been documented so many times that it has become accepted as normality.

The latest report on the subject at the time of writing, published by the Institute of Management (IM) in 1996 (Institute of Management, 1996), found that over half of managers reported they suffer from work overload, compared with just over a third in 1993. Ninety per cent of respondents commented that this increased level of stress affected their morale, health and work effectiveness; 84 per cent of managers in the survey work in excess of their official working week, with 60 per cent always doing this. Half the respondents took work home and over four in ten work at weekends. The worst hit are junior managers, with only 9 per cent of those asked looking forward to going to work and only 7 per cent feeling in control of their jobs.

While routine office politics and unreasonable deadlines account for some of this stress, one of the biggest sources of pressure cited by correspondents was the unreasonable strain placed on their work units by excessive stripping out of administrative cadres. Four in ten managers in the survey stated they have to cope with the loss of key personnel. Some senior managers in the survey also stated that they were nominally responsible for up to 50 direct 'reports' and 10 different functions, making a mockery of conventional spans of control.

One senior HR practitioner in a leading international drinks and food company, for example, was responsible for graduate recruitment, designing and supervising MBA internships, creating diversity policy, supporting presentations of HR policy to investors and devising a learning organisation strategy – all on top of her mainstream job of supervising the development of the company's top 200 managers. 'It was not possible to pay more than lip service to most of these functions,' she says. 'Creativity can only stretch so far.'

The second problem is the lack of balance that currently exists between people's personal and professional lives. In the IM survey two-thirds of respondents commented that they do not manage to achieve a good balance between home and work; in addition the inability to find adequate time with their partner, to relax and for hobbies causes stress for over 60 per cent of managers.

Most of the attention about the imbalance between home and professional life has focused on the difficulties of managing childcare and routine household matters effectively – a quarter of female managers in the IM study found childcare a source of stress and 45 per cent of men were stressed by not seeing enough of their children.

However this is only one, albeit important, negative by-product of poorly thought out delayering. A survey by Roffey Park Management Institute in 1997 (Lammiman, Holbeche and Syrett, 1997) found that innovative boardroom decisions are often informed by ideas, concepts and experiences gained from activities outside senior managers' mainstream work – for example, work outside conventional hours as school governors, local councillors and charitable trustees;

information and ideas picked up from television, radio, non-work-related reading; routine social conversations with family members and family friends; and casual encounters with acquaintances on holidays, in trains or planes or at parties. The more managers are cut off from the world outside the company's immediate stakeholders, the report concluded, the less innovative and wide-ranging boardroom deliberations will prove.

Rover has also found that there is a direct link between the commitment employees at all levels are able to bring to their personal lives and the enthusiasm they bring to their work. John Allcock, manager of development and production at Rover's learning business division, commented in 1994 (Syrett, 1994):

> People are committed to things they perceive to be important in their lives – and you cannot force them to choose between one valued aspect of their lives and another. Some employers seem to design their working practices on the assumption that an individual's commitment to his work and the commitment he shows to his family and personal interests detract from one another. We believe, by contrast, that they reinforce each other. Helping people achieve a balanced home life is the surest way of increasing their contribution to the company.

All of these issues are directly related to the quality of the organisation's health – and by inference to the quality of its healthcare. The first aspect of the HR profession's new role as corporate physiologist is therefore the constant process of diagnosis, observation and monitoring that allows senior management to spot quickly where support is breaking down or is simply not there and where potentially dangerous viruses – in the form of discontent, demotivation and hostility – are lurking beneath the surface.

Christine Gaskell at Rolls-Royce places a premium on regular communication with team leaders and the company's 'associates'. While her schedule is hectic and regularly takes her off-site, she makes a point of walking around the factory twice a week. 'One of the principal reasons is so that we always have antennae out to ensure that people are not being left out by change or are feeling threatened and unable to voice this.'

Similarly, the various initiatives at Kent County Council in recent years, particularly the Making Connections programme (see below), were helped by the regular interventions of senior policy advisers, working immediately below the directors, of the major departments. These advisers played a significant role in breaking down old-fashioned, hierarchical systems and cultures by working 'below the surface'. In the words of Sally Rushworth, assistant director, strategic support, Highways and Transportation:

> There is a tendency to see formal schemes like Making Connections as the benchmark of whether an organisation is genuinely committed to change. But valuable as these benefits are, they are only a means to an end. It is what goes on in work units on a day to day basis that really matters.

Part of this role at Kent has been to 'sense' where there are problems in much the same way as Christine Gaskell does at Rolls-Royce. A further dimension, in an organisation where a masculine culture still permeates the senior levels, is to encourage staff to volunteer the fact when they need support. 'We are playing an increasingly important role in helping management to thinking holistically,' says Judy Oliver until recently head of professional support. 'When you employ someone they are not just bringing their skills but their feelings and emotions as well. It is helping to break down the old macho tradition that you shouldn't need to admit to needing help and should struggle on regardless.'

Clearly the use of staff surveys and focus groups has an important role to play in helping HR functions to observe, assess and diagnose – but it is important that their use is properly integrated into and reflects central aspects of new values that stem from the new structures created by the organisation.

For example, the issue of promoting a balanced lifestyle is as important to the jeans manufacturer Levi Strauss & Co as it is to Rover. In 1991 the company's commitment to promoting a work–home balance was taken a stage further in its European operations by the creation of a task force, modelled on a counterpart in the US, with representatives from five company locations. The main focus of the task force's work in the two years that followed was a Europe-wide survey to evaluate what employees required to achieve the balance they wanted.

The survey, distributed to 4,500 employees, confirmed that on the whole Levi Strauss & Co had less to worry about than many of its competitors. Overall, for example, less than a fifth of the company's workforce found difficulties in combining work and family responsibilities. Nevertheless, as a direct result of feedback it received from the survey, the company launched a series of initiatives to improve the working environment and conditions of its European workforce. These included:

- an employee assistance programme to deal with personal and career issues
- new flexible working practices, including: job sharing, time work, compressed weeks (Friday afternoon off)
- stress management programmes
- video conferencing (to reduce unnecessary business trips and therefore increase time at home)
- healthcare programmes
- leave of absence for childcare.

Dieter Schweinle, human resource director Europe, argues that investment in measures like these supports a long established company ethic that puts the personal needs of the workforce during times of change high on the boardroom agenda. He concludes:

> Our commercial success has stemmed partially from the fact that we have sustained a very strong set of values for over a century. We set ourselves very high standards and in doing so recognise that these will bring lasting benefits only if they are reflected in every aspect of our commercial activities and if they are applied across the whole company. From a very early part of our history we have been committed to helping our workforce achieve a balanced life. These latest measures show our European employees that this goal is still as strong as ever.

Similarly a leading UK insurance company, currently employing over 2,000 staff, has discovered imaginative ways to keep abreast of the feelings, thoughts and opinions of both its workforce and management during a period of intense change that has included a company-wide TQM initiative, successful applications for ISO 9000 certification by a number of different departments and a reappraisal of its key business processes.

The most important 'sensing and diagnostic' tool used by the company has been an executive forum which meets once a quarter to consider long-term issues, new concepts and the latest thinking, with the avowed aim to make the senior management group 'fit for the year 2005'. Although the Forum was designed primarily to enable members to 'raise their heads above the parapets' by exposing them to new thinking and good management practice, it has also provided a neutral environment, away from the immediate strategic concerns of the organisation, where senior management can test the mood of the heads of their departments and profit centres.

The Forum, for example, uncovered the fact that department heads did not identify closely with the missions and values of the company, as formally stated in the company's literature. As a direct result, a new set of missions and values was drawn up in collaboration with department heads. The Forum also highlighted that effective team-working was being undermined by a 'culture of politeness' that made it hard for people to place difficult issues on the table. A working party was set up, headed by the manager who had chaired the meeting of the Forum, to examine ways in which this could be improved.

Finally, the Forum revealed that, while the way in which key processes were being redesigned was effective and that the employment conditions and welfare of the staff was above average compared with other local companies, more needed to be undertaken to involve and motivate staff at all levels. This was confirmed by a specially commissioned MORI poll which showed that confidence in senior executives was not as high as the strategic management group would have liked. Once again, the company is currently seeking ways to rectify this.

'These are all matters concerning good corporate health,' says the company's personnel director. 'We have good reason to be proud of our track record in the insurance industry and our commercial performance is as good as we would wish it to be. But we have to look ahead and the more we leave any discontent lurking below the surface the more it is likely to jump up and bite us when we least expect it.'

Assessment, prognosis and treatment

Devolution and decentralisation, coupled with more complex organisational structures, now make it hard to deliver solutions to common people problems that are applicable across the board. As we have already examined in Chapter 1, different parts of the organisation are often in contrasting situations. It is perfectly possible these days to find one department or profit centre reducing their headcount or outsourcing their operations for efficiency reasons while another is actively engaged in a major recruitment operation.

Equally, due to entirely local factors, the management team in one department might be highly motivated due to the inspired leadership style of the team or project leader while another located within 25 metres of the first is demoralised, with key individuals currently looking outside the company for another job. The Nicola Horlick crisis at Deutsche Morgan Grenfell (see page 36) was caused partially because confidence in senior management had been undermined by a management purge in the company's unit trust business the previous year that had affected Horlick's department disproportionately compared with their counterparts just down the corridor.

It is tempting to conclude, then, that the role of the HR practitioner is to assess and treat *local* ailments wherever they occur – and that in this sense the HR function has been decentralised along with everybody else. In one organisation cited by Polly Kettley in a recent report by the Institute of Employment Studies (Kettley, 1995), the training and development department was fundamentally restructured. Previously there were some 25 personnel and training staff with four levels of hierarchy for each of the area offices. The lower graded training staff did most of the delivery while higher graded staff determined training needs. These highly differentiated roles, Kettley stressed, proved too inflexible for the very different needs of individual branches. Consequently the function was reduced by a third and reorganised into just two grades. Every trainer is now responsible for delivery, development of new materials and training needs analysis for the named branches they serve.

In other firms, the HR function has become close to the business it serves by adopting a matrix system. Here personnel professionals hold responsibility for a particular professional specialism (employee relations, reward, HRD), and also for meeting the full range of needs of an area or division.

Yet at the same time the most fundamental principle of effective delayering, particularly if it is connected directly with a TQM or BPR initiative, is that everyone in the organisation subscribes to a similar set of values and aims and supports the changes with the right behaviour. Encompassing both a treatment (strategic plan), remedy (mission) and cure (vision), this essentially HR response to the breakdown in corporate muscle that often occurs in the wake of excessive downsizing or delayering requires a strategic perspective that encompasses the entire organisation.

The almost universal introduction of tailored company-wide values in restoring a company's morale following restructuring, or as the foundation for a TQM initiative, makes this potentially one of the most important strategic HR contributions. The most recent externally reported example (Clarke, Hooper and Nicholson, 1997) was the role of the HR function in helping to transform Lloyds of London following its crash in the early 1990s.

Corporate restructuring was the first stage. The HR function replaced the existing 16 job grades with five wide bands and linked pay to performance appraisals. It also introduced a redundancy programme that cut the workforce by 15 per cent.

It then had to develop and encourage the behaviour required to make the new-look company a success. Chris Hooper, manager of remuneration and HR planning commented in a recent article in *People Management*:

> We wanted staff to focus on satisfying their customers in the market rather than their bosses in the corporation, and on the results of their work rather than on the task itself. And we wanted them to learn from their own mistakes instead of seeking scapegoats. The organisation had to switch from a command-and-control system to one that encouraged employees to create value, rather than simply to meet budgets and avoid risks.

To underpin a culture change programme that the Lloyds' HR team

Table 4 *Lloyds' core values*

- goal orientation
- competitiveness and profitability
- the customer
- innovation and responsiveness to change
- high quality work
- positiveness and openness
- cooperation
- individual accountability
- commitment and adaptability
- integrity

Source: Clarke *et al.*, 1997

were keen to focus on tangible business objectives, they identified 10 core values that described the management culture that was needed (see Table 4). These were tested using six focus groups, involving 50 employees from all parts and levels of the corporation. These not only allowed the HR team to make important adjustments but highlighted participants capable of being champions of change who were subsequently trained as facilitators for a series of workshops that become the core of the entire process.

Among our own case-studies, the example of Birse Construction (see page 48) illustrates very clearly the consequences of a piecemeal approach to people management in a delayered company. Rapid expansion, leading to piecemeal recruitment from contractors and competitors, gradually eroded a culture based on integrity and customer care. The only solution, very similar to that of Lloyds, was a 'sheepdip' programme encompassing over 1,000 managers and employees supported by a company-wide staff appraisal system and a set of personal development plans. The important part, the company stresses, was that everyone was involved, promoting a sense of 'we are all in it together'. When British Rail tried a similar approach, it failed because because managers did not have to take part; the staff concluded that managers did not think they needed to modify their behaviour.

The strategic role played by the manager responsible for implementing the programme, Steve French, shows how important it is for

HR practitioners to retain both a strategic perspective and a close relationship with the board. In his words:

> Unusually for a company in the construction industry, I was called 'culture director'. The conventional idea is that anyone in an HR role merely communicates company policy. However I led the programme from the start and although I had the backing of the CEO and Chairman, there was very little convincing to be done. I had been safety director and had close ties to the people that mattered.

Blind trial, controlled trial

The key to the success of the Lloyds' change programme was the work of the focus groups comprising employees from all parts of the organisation. This provided the HR team with a number of important front-line perspectives through a system of ratings backed up by comments and examples.

Feedback from the groups showed that there was no widespread concept of service, although people accepted the need to improve. Managers did not empower, consult or delegate enough; decision making took too long; and there was a powerful sense among staff of 'them and us' – although it was acknowledged that individual accountability was increasing. There were also barriers between departments and between the corporation and the market, leading to inconsistency, duplication and a lack of cooperation. There was hardly any career guidance and the new performance management system was having teething problems.

'The criticisms were extremely honest for an organisation that had in the past found it difficult to face facts,' say Jane Clarke and John Nicholson, directors of the business psychology consultancy Nicolson McBride, which helped Lloyds implement the change programme. 'Ensuring these feelings were openly expressed was so important to Lloyds that it promised to keep participants' identities confidential. We even made the gesture of tearing up the list of participants' names.'

The feedback enabled the HR team to readjust the approach of the series of two-day workshops which were central to the change programme and to which all employees were invited. What clinical physiologists would term blind or controlled trials are important in all initiatives designed to change or influence behaviour because of the gulf that often exists between the perspective of senior management and that of front-line workers.

Trials of this type are also well suited to delayered organisations, enabling new methods of working to be piloted in one part of the firm before being applied elsewhere or universally. At Kent County Council, arguably the most decentralised of our case examples, the introduction of team-based pay was successfully introduced following the conducting of a pilot award scheme, from October 1994 to the end of March 1995, covering the small head office management team within the Adult Education Service. The pilot aimed to identify the benefits and pitfalls of team reward based on the council's own practical experience.

In designing the scheme, the five members of the head office team addressed a number of key areas seen as crucial to the development of team pay, if it was to fit in with Kent County Council's culture, help improve performance and be capable of being extended to other teams within the authority:

- a method of defining the team which took into account the time spent by members on the team's work and the consistency of the work aims of each member with those of the rest of the team
- the criteria used for team awards, which enabled teams to have a good understanding of how KCC's performance management scheme worked and which fostered openness and trust between members
- a validation process capable of confirming whether or not the team's perception of its performance was accurate and which placed its performance in the context of other teams
- a method of setting targets which measured team performance and helped focus on future planning.

During the pilot scheme, monitoring took place on a monthly basis, linked to the established cycle of head office management meetings. Participants rated, on a 1–10 basis key issues such as: how far have the accountabilities of the team been met? How far have the team's targets been met for the year? How well has the team developed a clear plan, communicated it to others and measured performance against it? And how good has the team's decision-making ability been? The monthly assessments helped chart the team's performance until a final performance assessment in mid-February 1995.

In addition to having a very positive effect on team members, the pilot scheme highlighted the benefits and flaws of the approach to team-based pay Kent wanted to adopt. On the plus side, team targets encouraged a greater understanding of the team's role and helped establish a common agenda; monitoring performance led to a more structured approach to team meetings, which in turn helped team members cope more effectively with change and the unexpected; and a team award brought with it a better sense of reward and was more motivating than individual performance pay, which was potentially divisive.

On the down side, team awards needed the full commitment of all members and fostered low morale if this did not occur; agreeing accountabilities and setting targets was very time consuming; external validation of a team's performance was hard to organise; and a high level of training was needed to ensure the scheme worked effectively.

Reassessing, supporting, counselling, 'applying balm'

Kent County Council also discovered that however professional and effective piloting is before any major HR initiative, there is a constant need for reassessment and re-evaluation. The process of devolving responsibility for local budgets which was started in the late 1980s unleashed a revolution that initially left local managers unsupported. As Mike Dudding says:

> To some extent, we went too far. People started coming back to head office and commenting that they would like some boundaries to work around and some guidelines and sources of advice

Table 5 *Extract from Kent County Council corporate framework*

If my responsibilities include:	What are my 'must-dos'?	Who is there to help me?
Purchasing	• secure rational, effective and 'value for money' purchasing decisions, within the legal constraints applicable to a public sector organisation • adhere to the Purchaser Framework, KCC Standing Orders, Financial Regulations, EC and UK Legislation • ensure that compliance with the Code of Practice for Tenders and Contracts is secured and maintained	List of departmental purchasers
Commitee reports (the decision-making process)	Ensure that: • the Committee or Chief Officer has the delegated authority to take the decision sought • procedures imposed by legislation and KCC Standing Orders are complied with • the action proposed is legal and authorised by an Act of Parliament	List of departmental committee contacts
Computers	Comply with: • law on security, data protection, computer misuse and software copyright • KCC policy on procurement, security, health and safety • requirements for investment appraisal of key new developments and post-implementation reviews • reporting requirements to enable Members and the IS Head of Profession to oversee the IS function	List of departmental IS managers

If my responsibilities include:	**What are my 'must-dos'?**	**Who is there to help me?**
Property	Comply with: • legislative requirements, KCC policy and good practice on the acquisition, management and disposal of property, and particularly of the 'notional lease' (as detailed in the Functional Framework, Section 7) • legislative requirements and good practice on the use and occupation of property • KCC policy, good practice and legislative requirements in obtaining property services	List of departmental property managers

Source: Kent County Council, 1997

which met the questions 'what can I do, what can't I do and, if I get stuck, where do I go for help?'

To meet these needs a team at head office comprising representatives of the key resource functions, headed by Dudding, developed a management handbook spelling out the key functions of each local manager (see Table 5). The preamble to the handbook reads:

> The primary objective of this handbook is to give a clear definition of the policies and practices within which we should all operate as managers of a single organisation. It sets the context, and standards where appropriate, within which our individual department-based procedures are applied.
>
> Changes in our organisation have had an effect on the accountability and responsibility among staff. Here we explain what this means to you in practice and provide basic guidelines to help you understand your role more clearly. You will find the answers to many common questions and there are also references to more technical and specialist documents and other sources of advice.
>
> Theory has been largely set aside in favour of practical advice

> and the content of each section assumes that the reader has little previous knowledge of the material. Some managers may find, therefore, that they are already quite familiar with some of the sections. Where more specialist references are already available these are signposted in the text rather than reproduced.

The handbook is very similar in its aims to one produced for local line managers by the Hong Kong Government as part of a major culture change exercise undertaken in the years immediately prior to the transfer of sovereignty.

At the time – and this case example is clearly historical – the Government, as part of the reforms initiated by Governor Chris Patten, had launched a major public campaign 'Serving the Community' which bound civil servants to be guided by the four aims of 'being accountable', 'living within our means', 'managing for performance' and 'developing a culture of service'.

In many ways, the overall initiative – and the role of the HR function in sponsoring it – mirrored that of Lloyds' change management programme. Management layers were cut by half and the HR team leading the programme developed, with senior civil servants, ten values which reflected the aims of the Serving the Community initiative. These were:

- Openness
- Partnership
- Foresight
- Leadership
- Effectiveness
- Propriety
- Commitment
- Integrity
- Courtesy
- Responsiveness.

The next stage was to develop competencies that supported these values and, not surprisingly, these placed a high premium on devolution, empowerment and self-development. Similarly to KCC, local managers needed significant help in achieving the change in management style, particularly in a culture where top-down management is still commonplace and front-line staff are used to highly defined roles with little or no discretion.

The HR team produced a detailed handbook to support line managers' new tasks. A running theme throughout the text was how to manage a relationship with staff based on a regular appraisal of not only their performance but their training and career needs. The team also facilitated training and consultancy support for the local training needs of specific departments. For example, the geotechnical department 'bought in' a series of workshops on TQM processes to underpin their own quality initiative – this was a particular priority because public interest in the work of the department reached a new high in the mid-1990s following a series of landslides and consequent criticisms about slope safety, for which the department was responsible.

Evaluation, reassessment and support is thus the aspect of the HR practitioner's role where the tension between centralised control and local discretion, and the retention and devolution of key HR functions, is most fraught.

KCC's Mike Dudding argues that HR practitioners need to be very adept networkers to maintain the balance:

> In any lean organisation, there are formal and informal structures. What we try to acknowledge is that both exist. The formal structure says that from tomorrow Ted Bloggs will no longer be in the finance department, but will become a local finance officer working in Highways and Transportation at one of its area offices. The informal fact of the matter, though, is that he will continue to network on a regular basis with his former colleagues who now work in other service departments such as Education Services or Arts and Libraries. We have to know how to recognise and acknowledge the 'soft matrix' and use it to our advantage.

Equally Rolls-Royce's Christine Gaskell stresses that in any initiative that is originated by HR from the centre but devolved to the line, HR practitioners need to exercise a high degree of self-imposed modesty.

> I had a lot of concerns about the introduction of a team culture and, more particularly, about the recruitment of a new layer of

> zone managers, because it was initially too personnel driven and, more to the point, seen to be personnel driven. We cannot own the process because then you do not get the buy in from your internal customer.
>
> Personnel should not have and do not need the plaudits. We have a strong customer focus: we only do things that are valued by our customers. If these services are not valued, they are not worth doing. The only reason we exist is because they think we are relatively useful.

Personal trainer, physiotherapist, lab technician

Gaskell's comments bring us back to the long standing debate about which functions should be devolved or retained by a cut down HR function – and whether the HR function will survive at all in an age of leanness.

The final clutch of functions – those that relate most closely to the personal trainer and physiotherapist in terms of an athlete – undoubtedly need to take place in a lean firm. If the experiences of Rolls-Royce Motor Cars, Lloyds, Kent County Council and the Hong Kong Government show anything, it is that if you devolve responsibility, the people picking it up need to be trained in new skills and require regular appraisal and guidance.

In most organisations, the line manager or supervisor plays the role of the physiotherapist, identifying problems of morale and the need for further training. This was particularly the case among line managers in the Hong Kong Government. Increasingly the role of personal trainer is contracted out – to external consultants, business school tutors and specialists.

However, the people undertaking these roles need briefing, supervising and supporting. The link between initiatives taken at a local level and their impact on an overall change management strategy needs to be analysed and, if front-line training is to be conducted by external agents, the methods and concepts used by these agents need to be anchored closely to the needs of the company.

The Executive Forum run by a leading UK insurance company profiled on page 66 is a classic case in point. The initiative was aimed at the Top 40 Management Group of the company. The seminars were designed by external consultants and used external speakers ranging from leading thinkers from academic institutions to senior directors from non-competing companies. However, the personnel function played a leading role in ensuring that the topics chosen were closely linked to 'live' issues in the company and that the pre-course exercises and post-presentation discussions reflected the views and were couched in a language that members of the Forum would instantly recognise and relate to. It was the ability of the personnel director and the internal personnel consultant to link their inside knowledge of the company to an understanding of the learning design techniques being used by the consultants that made the Forum a success.

Two issues arise from this. First, while it is theoretically possible to outsource the entire HR function, the dangers are self-evident if this results in strategic HR functions being undertaken by people who are not knitted closely into the entire body of the organisation and lack the internal networks and corporate memory to shape strategic change management initiatives and to brief, supervise and monitor tactical HR measures taken at a local level.

Just as a physiologist would never prescribe treatments (drugs, diet, physiotherapy) without a detailed knowledge of an athlete's history and physical state, so an HR practitioner – or anyone responsible for key HR functions – should never initiate HR interventions that are not based on a detailed knowledge of the organisation's recent history and the current perspective of the workforce. Not all of this can be uncovered from the outside by clinical testing. As Mike Dudding from Kent County Council stresses on page 44, you need a knowledge of the informal networks, grapevines and 'soft' matrices and come from 'living' in the firm on a day-to-day basis.

Secondly, the most effective HR practitioners in the organisations we visited or the cases we examined, managed successfully the complex interface between the tactical and the strategic and the individual and the organisation. In the debate about leanness, too much emphasis has been placed on dealing with local issues and the cult of the individual. These things are important – in fact vital – but they should not be focused on at the expense of strategic initiatives and considerations that keep the corporate body as a whole in a state of peak health and which enable HR practitioners the freedom to shift resources so that muscle can be built where it is necessary. We shall explore this issue in more depth in Chapter 5.

5

Issues for the Future

The shelf-life of management concepts is very short these days. Womack's concept of lean production was the vogue in the early 1990s and already it has faded. This has a lot to do with the fact that many companies associated it, inaccurately, with cost cutting rather than building quality and with belt tightening in a recession rather than as a platform for growth during a boom economy.

We have already seen that this is not the case; a fit company flexing its muscles needs to retain its leanness. However, a number of emerging HR issues are likely to alter or transform thinking about leanness and this chapter explores these in more depth.

Leanness: a stairway to heaven or a game of snakes and ladders?

There is a strong inference in both the initial Warwick/Bath model and our own version of it (see Figures 1–4) that there is a step by step approach to leanness that starts ruthlessly and ends by placing the organisation in a state of Utopian bliss. Downsize, restructure, retrain, remotivate, empower and unleash are the business steps to heaven in most change management case-studies.

However life at the coalface, as ever, is not quite like this. In the first case, progress along the steps to ideal leanness often resembles a game of snakes and ladders rather than a celestial stairway. Let us take the case of British Airways. It would be difficult to find another corporate change management strategy that, until 1997, fitted the stage by stage model of leanness to fitness more closely. The first stage – leanness to cut costs – was achieved through 20,000 redundancies, the removal of 50 of the company's top 150 managers, rationalisation of the company's multifarious network of expensive insurance policies and the closing of prestigious but unnecessary central London premises.

The second stage – leanness to achieve efficiency – was achieved through the imaginative use of shifts among both ground staff and cabin crew and by the establishment of closer links with key suppliers such as the baggage handling staff employed by the airport authorities in countries where the company flew services. The third stage – leanness to support growth and innovation – was achieved by a series of customer focused programmes like 'Putting People First' and 'Fit for Business' which all staff attended in the run up to privatisation in 1987, which have helped instil the message that good service is everyone's responsibility.

In addition, during the two years since 1995, a new flexible approach to customer service has given front-line staff more discretion in the way they manage the staff–customer relationship. Cabin crew, for example, are no longer straitjacketed by guidelines that dictate the exact angle at which they hold the hors-d'oeuvres tray or which delicacy they should point to first. More importantly, at the behest of the crew themselves, the old rules that confined their responsibility to a fixed part of the aircraft – symbolised by the mantra 'not my aisle' (NMA) – has been replaced by the philosophy that any passenger's problem is your own. Indeed, NMA has become internal shorthand for the reforms that BA is making across the entire organisation.

All of this could not protect BA from the industry-wide equation of rising costs and falling revenue per passenger which, had things remained unchanged, would have resulted in the company making a loss by the year 2000. Unable to increase the number of passengers their planes carry or to price themselves out of the market by inflating fares, the only option left was to cut operational costs and, as we saw in Chapter 3, the resulting campaign has so far led to company-wide discontent and, at the time of writing, at least one strike. From being close to the celestial gates on the stairway to heaven, the company has tumbled back to the first rung. Unable to present the cuts along with a vision of a better land, as Lord King had in the early 1980s, the company offers very little reassurance that further redundancies might not be further down the line. Yet the negotiations that led to the strike took place at the same time that the company was undertaking a major marketing exercise to position itself as a global rather than a national airline, complete with a new livery and marketing slogan.

Leanness does not equal downsizing

The second point is that organisations that have successfully implemented Womack's concept of leanness do not necessarily begin by a major downsizing exercise. Leanness, as defined by Womack, requires firms to streamline and devolve their operations so that fewer employees are needed to get the same tasks done. This, according to Womack, releases talent to be used more effectively rather than providing employers with an excuse to lay off workers. Streamlining an operation to eliminate unnecessary processes and realign the remainder, therefore, may involve job cuts but equally might not – indeed, in many of the organisations that take lean ways of working seriously, such job cuts that do occur have very little to do with a stage by stage pathway to the kind of leanness Womack advocates.

At Kent County Council, for example, the process of delayering, decentralisation and devolution that took place in the late 1980s involved few significant cuts in personnel. Indeed in some cases, the need to support local managers effectively actually resulted in a temporary demand for greater professional resources.

As the outgoing deputy chief executive Ward Griffiths emphasises, the leanness came from a streamlined process: enabling staff to make decisions quickly and buy services on clients' or families' behalf with a minimum of red tape; encouraging a closer partnership to be established between service users, carers and providers; involving staff in quality assessment, so the service can plan and influence the style of existing and new provision; and increasing professional discipline in obtaining best value for money. 'Devolution has made staff more customer aware, more financially aware, more accountable and more able to management services within financial constraints,' he stresses.

Significant cuts have been made to the KCC workforce since the mid-1990s but, like British Airways, these have been for reasons that have little or nothing to do with a continuing internal desire for leanness as Womack defines it, and more to do with organisational changes imposed on the Council by outside agencies and external financial forces.

Because of local government reorganisation, the areas of Rochester and Gillingham in the County will form a Unitary Authority from 1998 and the Kent Fire Brigade will form a separate organisation as a combined fire authority funded by both Kent County Council and the new Unitary Authority.

The future Kent County Council, while still estimated to be one of the largest in the country, will be 15 per cent smaller by population and 5 per cent by area, and the successor county will need to be reorganised in order to maintain strategic direction and to provide good value for money in its delivery of services. At the time of writing, the Council was also grappling with a required reduction to its 1997/98 budget, which will inevitably involve staff reductions at all levels because, as one internal accounting report put it, 'each year it becomes increasingly difficult to find further efficiency opportunities and to avoid cuts in services'.

The cuts are all the more frustrating because, although the reorganisation will reduce the overall size and remit of the Council, the demands on its services will be more complex. In education, the new nursery voucher scheme (abandoned by the Labour Government) would have required sound administration to succeed, while social services care will need to be expanded if hospital waiting lists get longer or hospital policies change in order to discharge patients more quickly.

There will inevitably be a conflict between the need to reduce staffing levels to meet budget constraints and the need for staff to manage the change process involved in the reorganisation in addition to their usual tasks. As the Council's auditors Price Waterhouse pointed out in a report published towards the end of 1996, failure to manage staff reductions could jeopardise not only the implementation of organisational changes but also the quality of the provision of day-to-day services, as staff leave the organisation, either through early retirement, redundancy or to take up employment with the Unitary Authority.

Downsizing, upsizing

Kent County Council's dilemma in meeting the demands of its short-

Table 6 *Downsizing continues . . .*

Companies continue to eliminate jobs even as the economy enters its fourth year of expansion.

Date	Companies reporting job cuts (%)
1991	55.5
1992	46.1
1993	46.6
1994	47.3
1995	50

Source: American Management Association, 1996

Table 7 *. . . But it is accompanied by job creation*

Among the 50 per cent of companies that eliminated jobs in 1995, 60 per cent also created jobs at the same time.

Recruitment policy	Companies adopting this policy (%)
Eliminated jobs only	20
Neither created nor eliminated jobs	22
Created jobs only	28
Concurrently created and eliminated jobs	30

Source: American Management Association, 1996

term budgetary crisis while maintaining the management capacity to manage continuous change in the medium to long term is shared by many organisations in the late 1990s – and once again the trend has been set by North American firms.

Two-thirds of companies that cut jobs in a recent survey by the American Management Association (McNerney, 1996) also created jobs at the same time (see Tables 6 and 7). AMA's research director Eric Rolfe argues that this will soon be a common and perpetual situation for companies on both sides of the Atlantic. As he writes in the report accompanying the survey:

> What we are seeing is jobs being taken off the organisational chart because their functions are no longer necessary to the

> organisation, while new jobs are being added to the chart – jobs with different demands and somewhat different pay levels.
>
> As new technologies, new businesses and new competitive situations arise – and they do all the time – this re-examination of the business becomes perpetual. From time to time it may lead to a decision to eliminate jobs. From time to time it may lead to a decision to create jobs. And so the churning is constant and will remain a constant.

Ever the first sector of the UK economy to take its lead from North American HR practices, the City of London has shown that this trend is not confined to the other side of the Atlantic. A report published by a consortium of banks and investment houses in July 1997 (Rajan, 1997) predicted that a further 125,000 jobs in the financial services sector were at risk in the coming decade. At least as many new jobs would be created but they would require different baskets of skills. The report's author Amin Rajan of the Centre for Research and Technology in Europe commented: 'Far too much emphasis has been placed on industry knowledge and technical expertise and too little on personal attributes like self-reliance and the ability to network effectively.'

So what about careers?

In such demanding and unstable conditions, where jobs are no longer cut purely because of current market conditions, few companies believe, privately, they can offer employment security any more. They fear that what happened to British Airways in 1997 – an unforeseeable event such as changing market conditions, new competition or new technology – could force them to cut jobs to save profits at any time and in any circumstances, and that these lay offs will continue in stable economic conditions when the company is taking on new staff in other parts of its operations, making the cuts difficult to explain or justify to the unions or the workforce.

In these circumstances, one of the most important tasks remaining to the HR function – career management and development – has had to undergo a brutal reappraisal. In the 1994 survey conducted by Roffey Park Management Institute (Holbeche, 1994 and 1995), both line and HR managers used carefully crafted phrases, such as the need for staff to adopt 'a more flexible approach to careers and a more holistic view of development', and to appreciate 'the widest concept of career development' to acknowledge the fact that conventional career planning is being rendered obsolete by the brutalities of market driven business priorities.

Top of survey author Linda Holbeche's own list of recommendations on the HR role in career development is to 'manage expectations and help people to redefine their career expectations'. It is better to be honest and admit that upward career progression is a hopeless prospect for most employees, Holbeche argues, than perpetuate false expectations which, when they are inevitably disappointed, breed a cynicism that is counterproductive to productivity and morale.

Which brings us back to the notion of employability. As we highlighted in Chapter 1, employability has growing potential at a time when most young people entering the employment market have few of the expectations of job security and conventional career progression held by their parents. However, to make the employers' side of the bargain good, HR practitioners need to invest time and money in activities that have very little to do with the corporate bottom line.

Self-development: opening Pandora's box?

The implication behind the employability 'deal' is that the employer will provide the individual with some form of systematic self-development to build and enrich 'life' skills while he or she is an employee of the organisation.

Whether this is seen by employees as a genuine attempt by the organisation to live up to its side of the bargain, or just a cosmetic and cynical PR exercise, depends on how senior managers confront the following issues:

- *Eligibility* Is self-development a perk or a right? Is it open to everyone or just a small elite of managers, graduates and professionals? What will the organisation deem as 'acceptable' training? Will it include personal development which extends beyond the current job requirements? What effect is this likely to have on training budgets?

- *Appraisal* Asking employees to direct their own careers implies they know what you think they are capable of. This requires effective feedback of performance and appraisal. Is the organisation's current assessment procedure good enough to talk about openly or will it simply show up bias and inappropriate criteria for appraisal?
- *Counselling and careers advice* Opportunities for self-development will lead to a demand for better counselling and advice. Who will provide it? Is it better to use staff from a central personnel unit – who will have an accurate overview of opportunities in the organisation but who may seem remote – or external consultants who are more geared up to the task but are less well informed?
- *Internal labour markets* Once the organisation has created a dialogue with employees, better internal communications will be needed to advertise new jobs and career opportunities. What philosophy should govern the process? Is it better to take the conservative route and keep the process closed – so that the individual's aspirations are fed secretly (if at all) into the shortlisting process? Or should organisations go the whole way and let all staff apply for any jobs *they* think themselves suitable for?

The extraordinary reality about the late-1990s labour market seems to be this. Loyalty and commitment from the workforce are essential if companies wish to retain their capacity to innovate and continuously improve the quality of their customer service. Frederick Reichheld, director of the US consultancy Bain & Co, commenting about his work with Fortune 500 companies on how to retain their key customers, recently commented (Reichheld, 1997):

> We could not progress beyond a superficial treatment of customer loyalty without delving into employee loyalty. There is a cause and effect relationship between the two: it is impossible to maintain a loyal customer base without loyal employees; and

> the best employees prefer to work for companies that deliver the kind of superior value that builds customer loyalty.

At the same time, the prospect of continuous restructuring means that the levers that employers used to rely on to win a loyal workforce – a guarantee of employment security, the prospect of regular promotion, a favourable pension scheme – are no longer on offer. This seems to matter less to young people entering the job market now than to their parents – they do not see a job for life as a normality anyway – but what they will not stomach is being led on.

Organisations that hold out career prospects they know are unlikely to materialise, or rely on the employability deal without investing any resources to ensure that they fulfil their side of the bargain, invariably suffer greater attrition and wastage than those that are honest but genuinely attempt to ensure that time spent with the firm is time well spent in terms of the individual's long-term career.

HR practitioners have a key role to play in communicating the strategic purpose behind any restructuring, in advocating means to close the gap between the organisation's professed vision and actual practice (for example in managerial styles, reward and recognition, and career development), in ensuring that the corporate mission and values mean more to employees than a piece of paper on the company noticeboard (for example in linking value statements to managerial behaviour), and in fostering open and honest communication from the top down.

Lean versus virtual

In performing their role as communicators and clarifiers, the HR profession will also start to pick apart the delicate relationship between the lean and the virtual firm. Invisible but transcending even the matrix structures created by a lean strategy (see Figure 8), new virtual networks have been created by the greater use of e-mail, discussional databases like Lotus Notes and dedicated Intranet systems.

The very culture of the cross-boundary or boundaryless working systems that have been introduced to underpin lean working has also

Figure 8
The Changing Internal Network of Organisations

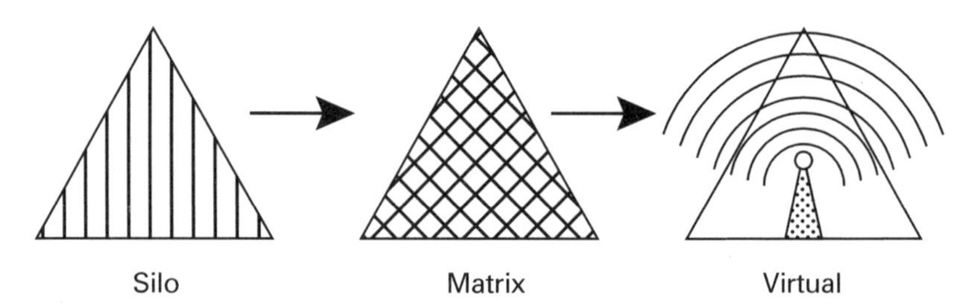

Source: Syrett and Lammiman, 1997

helped to fuel virtual networks and this is likely to be boosted still further by the redesign of processes to foster a free flow of information and ideas that has been prompted by the mid-1990s' concepts of knowledge management and organisational learning.

Internal computer-based communications have enfranchised the informal networks that lie beneath the corporate hierachy and shape the day-to-day life of the company. We saw in Chapter 1 how US firms like IBM use the key figures in these networks to spread the good and bad news – a bit like government officials use off the record briefings with lobby correspondents to communicate unattributable public policy. The gossip in the corridors which proves the main medium for the current company 'line' on any issue is increasingly being supplemented by Intranet surfing (see page 107).

In this sense leanness and virtuality have gone hand in hand, supported by the same forces that have helped to break down silo thinking and functional working. In an era when management no longer controls or supervises day-to-day work, internal virtual networks, far from being a threat to the work of the HR function, provide a new medium to perform one of its most important functions.

In a lean structure where there is greater devolution and decentralisation, computer-based communications also provide a new and provocative vehicle for professional and management education.

Standard Chartered Bank has run a highly successful in-company MBA programme since the early 1990s which has played a large role in helping the company move from an expatriate-based management culture to one based on a global perspective. Twice yearly, participants from as far afield as Harare, Kuala Lumpur and Manchester meet for residential seminars. The rest of the year they stay in touch with each other via the Internet, conducting group exercises and study projects over the World-Wide Web. All materials on the programme are available on-line, giving participants more control over their learning methods.

Will virtuality wind up supplanting leanness? The prospect is unlikely, at least in the foreseeable future. Most companies that have redesigned their processes to foster free flows of information and ideas between employees place a premium on the tactile language that can be exchanged only through direct human contact (see the examples of BMW and Oticon in Chapter 1, pages 15–18).

Dominic Swords, the manager at Henley Management College responsible for running the Standard Chartered programme, stresses that the degree of intimacy participants maintain over the Internet is only possible because of the bonding that takes place during the bi-annual residential courses:

> The holy grail for us is to bring about an imaginative interaction between participants, which leads to effective problem solving and the development of new ideas. We use residential courses to undertake teambuilding and cross-cultural work, including outdoor activities. The lesson we are learning again and again is that sophisticated learning over the Web, and indeed any other form of productive interchange, can only be fostered through an initial face to face encounter.

Europe: who's learning from whom?

It now seems clear that the Labour Party, at least under the leadership of Tony Blair, is unlikely to bring back the kind of employment legislation that in the 1970s made it impossible to practise lean ways of working. Indeed at the Amsterdam Summit in June 1997 the newly elected Mr Blair was almost Thatcher-like in his support of the flexible labour market.

Certain aspects of European social legislation may seem problematic on paper but rarely impose an unbearable burden on employers with the kind of HR practices advocated by apostles of leanness. The working hours directive is a good case in point. British business looks especially vulnerable to a regulation setting rules for annual holidays (four weeks starting in 1999), breaks (after every six hours), rest periods (11 hours a day and at least one complete day a week) and night shifts (averaging no more than eight hours). A quarter of the UK's workers in fact work more than 48 hours a week and about 40 per cent get less than four weeks' holiday. A range of businesses in which demand is seasonal or unpredictable – hotels and print shops respectively – work longer shifts than the new rules allow.

However, as with many other European regulations, the loopholes are as elaborate as the rules. The directive does not apply at all to workers in transport and sea fishing, or to doctors in training. Managers and other decision makers can be exempted from everything except the annual holiday provision. Government can shield several industries including agriculture, media and utilities from most of the provisions. And workers in other industries can escape through collective agreements.

For the most part the directive will fall hardest on small companies with slapdash record keeping and large numbers of seasonal part-time and temporary workers. It will favour companies which retain collective bargaining procedures and, in this respect, it will also transfer limited power back to the unions. However, if you take Womack's leading principle – that lean production can only yield benefits with a committed workforce – then apart from an increased burden on personnel record keeping there is little in the directive that will cause you to lose sleep at night.

Whatever the thrust of European social legislation, European employers are introducing many of the changes advocated by the lean revolution – and it is this that will, in the long run, determine the rigidity or flexibility of the European labour market. In Germany for example, car manufacturers like Opel and Audi have pioneered lean production, and the number of production workers operating in cross-functional teams, although small by comparison with Japan and America, has risen steadily from only 4 per cent in 1990 to nearly a quarter (Roth, 1995). In France the public utilities Electricité de France and Gaz de France, employing between them 145,000, have combined to modernise their core businesses to bring them into line with a more open, competitive, decentralised and international marketplace. A key part of the process has been the introduction of cross-functional teams with defined targets to support a change from a culture which has traditionally been product-oriented and national in its perspective to one which is customer-oriented and international in its outlook.

6

Developing an HR Strategy for Fitness

If fitness in an organisation requires a proactive HR function which is closely involved in shaping as well as responding to corporate strategy, what issues are most likely to require a coherent HR response? Drawing on the experiences of the organisations we interviewed, four imperatives stand out.

Behaviour

The lean revolution superseded the quality revolution in placing behaviour at the top of the HR agenda. The twin purposes of restructuring the workforce into cross-functional teams and the establishment of a culture of continuous improvement require the wholehearted cooperation of the workforce. More recent management concepts associated with lean ways of working – organisational learning, knowledge management, empowerment – are all founded on the need for employees to feel sufficiently motivated and enthusiastic about their work to use their hidden reserve of talent for the benefit of the organisation rather than devoting it solely to their personal interests and family life, and, linked with this, to demonstrate certain required types and standards of behaviour in their relationships with colleagues, suppliers, contractors, customers and other key stakeholders.

The best organisations have become very systematic in the ways in which they have identified the behaviour they wish their staff to demonstrate. Rolls-Royce Motor Cars have incorporated new standards of behaviour into the competency framework they have developed to provide selection criteria against which they are recruiting a new layer of zone managers. An exercise of this kind typically involves preliminary surveys and assessments of supervisory and managerial staff involving 360-degree appraisal in order to identify the gap between existing and required behaviour, and subsequent training and development programmes to support newly recruited staff. In the case of Rolls-Royce the competency framework they developed for zone managers is now being used as a model for other parts of the organisation and, as the director of personnel Christine Gaskell comments, it is having an important impact on the company's culture:

> Changing a culture is not just a matter of doing things differently, it is ensuring that people behave differently. How people perform against the competency framework, and not as before how they did at the technical interview, is now the deciding factor in the assessment process.

Other companies have been re-examining individual career needs given the fragility of the psychological contract in an era of almost continuous restructuring. The first type of initiative has been to create new internal careers in the wake of horizontal work structures that have all but eliminated traditional career paths. As part of the US car giant Chrysler's move towards lean production, for example, the company revamped its purchasing system and deployed cross-functional 'platform' teams, each focusing on developing one line of cars or trucks.

Until recently members of these teams, most of whom have been permanently removed from their former functional 'home', were content to be part of a process that has enjoyed clear and positive results. But they are now becoming anxious about their lack of career path and progression and the dilution of their skills due to lack of communication with colleagues elsewhere in the company. Chrysler has responded by systematically alternating them between team assignments and functional assignments and by making every primary production worker a 'process expert' through continuous training in lean techniques.

A further group are using a variety of means to help individuals 'own' their own careers in an attempt both to fulfil their part of the employability contract (see Chapters 3 and 5) and to combat the isolation many employees feel in work groups set up in flatter organisational structures. ICL, for example, is using self-managed learning 'sets' to help employees increase their sense of personal value and encourage a dual emphasis on learning and personal responsibility. Each learning set, aided by a set adviser, consists of groups of individuals who each develop their own learning objectives, usually tied to their work objectives, and then seek help from other members in achieving these objectives. At ICL, attendance at set meetings is assigned the same value as other business meetings. Similar initiatives in other organisations, which have been supported by resource guides, learning resource centres and the use of mentors drawn from the ranks of the line managers, have aimed to encourage employees to self-manage their lives, take stock of their experiences and accomplishments, make commitment to themselves and others to find ways of changing their behaviour, and to test their new behaviour by seeking feedback either through a supervisor or formal mentor. The objective of nearly all these initiatives has been to make career development a joint responsibility, with the planning process – involving occupational choice, self-development and the development of job assignments – taken over by the individual.

Finally there is a potential role for process redesign in influencing organisational behaviour. One of the characteristics of companies that have used lean structures to support growth and innovation has been the redesign of processes in such a way that they do not only break down interdepartmental barriers and foster regular communication between cross-disciplinary teams but also encourage individuals to use their own initiative in seeking new solutions by cutting through less immediately obvious 'Chinese walls'.

BMW's concept of a 'flow of ideas' to complement the more traditional Japanese concept of a flow of materials at their R&D plant in Munich (see Chapter 1) is an example of this. We have already seen that the sequence followed in the design and development of new cars was used as the basis for the layout of the complex, ensuring that design engineers have easy access to technical planners and that staff from design offices can communicate easily with their opposite numbers in the model workshops and the pilot assembly line.

The active encouragement of serendipity in the building is based on MIT research suggesting that casual face-to-face conversations generate the highest yield of new ideas and that the flow of these is most likely to be interrupted by barriers such as doors, telephones, long corridors, stairways and journeys to other buildings.

However, since moving into the new complex, BMW have taken the concept of 'ideas flow interruption' a stage further. The development of prototype components has always been a time consuming and expensive affair. Specific instruments need to be developed to manufacture the component and if the prototype is abandoned the instruments have to be scrapped as well. The cost and time involved discourage wild experimentation of the type that sometimes leads to major breakthroughs – so BMW introduced laser moulded plastic as a new material for prototypes. Because the cost of failure is now so low, the volume of ideas has increased fourfold.

In like manner, Lars Kolind (see Chapter 1) significantly increased the flow of information and knowledge throughout Oticon by a two-fold strategy that not only reconfigured the organisation into project groups of multi-skilled workers but also discouraged formal meetings and paper communication in favour of casual encounters. Workers throughout the organisation are encouraged to come up with their own ideas and suggestions how to improve their work and then implement the solutions after having involved those people who would be impacted by the change. 'The emphasis', comments Lars Kolind, 'is on encouraging everyone to seek out the right person whenever they have a problem or solution.'

The role of management

The lean revolution has also brought about the biggest change in the role of managers since their present role emerged at the turn of the century.

Three emerging roles are significant. The first is interface management. As outplacement and contract working has become more commonplace, line managers in the front line are adjusting to the unfamiliar role of briefing, coordinating and monitoring the activities of consultants and contractors, and in some cases overseeing the objectives of work units made up of employees who have a direct and conventional contractual relationship with the host organisation and consultants or contract staff who do not.

As we saw in Chapter 2, there needs to be a clear definition of boundaries governing which functions are retained in-house and which are to be outsourced. In addition there need to be integrated points of control supported by legal agreements, social ties and shared values. In some cases this will require line managers to sit on a joint review body set up to deal with difficult issues and/or establishing a close working relationship with account managers working for the supplier, exchanging information about each other's business, and reviewing the long-term development of each project.

The second emerging role of managers is to design and oversee the new processes that are needed to communicate with and supervise the new internal part-time and temporary workforce that makes up anything between a third and a half of most organisations' human resources.

Radical changes to when and where staff work pose a number of important issues surrounding day-to-day communication and control. In particular:

- how and where they are briefed and allocated work
- how they will liaise and communicate with colleagues inside the organisation
- how decisions taken by staff working new patterns of work will affect other people's work
- how they will liaise and communicate with people outside the organisation (customers, clients, suppliers, etc)
- how their work will be monitored and assessed
- how office space and facilities will be allocated.

It is not within the remit of this book to cover all of these issues in depth but the scope and breadth of the changes that may be necessary can be illustrated by looking at two aspects of flexible working – the contractual and logistical task of managing reporting and monitoring procedures; and the psychological aspects of induction and integration.

The introduction of new work patterns will increase the need for effective reporting procedures. This is particularly true for workers outside the office (networkers, teleworkers, homeworkers, etc) but also for any form of working arrangement where employees are expected to take greater responsibility for their day-to-day workload (such as job sharers and professional part-timers).

Systems to monitor a worker's output could include fixed meetings on a regular basis to set objectives, negotiate success criteria, monitor progress and adjust deadlines; daily telephone reporting at fixed hours of the day and more imaginative use of e-mail; and regular days on which workers are expected to work on-site.

In certain circumstances, the requirement for off-site workers to keep in regular contact with their supervisors or managers should be built into the contract. Meetings or briefings should be fixed well in advance and take into account workers' domestic and personal circumstances (for example, the requirement of working mothers without childcare facilities to deliver and fetch their children to and from school). When allocating work, duties should be broken up into easily defined and measurable tasks, projects or objectives. Achievement of these responsibilities should be broken down into set deadlines according to an agreed timetable. Regular review dates should be incorporated to identify problems early on and adjust deadlines if appropriate. The balance between on-site and off-site working should be carefully reviewed to ensure that workers keep in touch with essential colleagues; have access to professional facilities (libraries, databases, copying equipment etc); and do not become isolated and therefore demotivated. A key factor in the early success of the Rank Xerox networking scheme was the regular visits by off-site workers to their local offices, to review their work but also to keep in touch with the organisation's mainstream activities.

Equal attention should be paid to building an effective psychological contract between the individual and the organisation; this is, if anything, more important in the case of part-time, temporary and contract staff than with their 'core' colleagues. Seemingly trivial things like ensuring that non-core staff are represented in staff associations, extending staff facilities to them (sports facilities, staff outings, discounts etc), and reporting their activities, achievements and interests in house journals will have the psychological effect of making them feel accepted as full members of the organisation even though they are not working full-time or on-site. The professional and social contact they will gain with other employees will enable them to build good personal networks and break down much of the traditional hostility they might otherwise encounter from colleagues.

The conventional complaint that part-time staff lack motivation and leave early is frequently caused by their complete failure to identify with the organisation. Too often this is the organisation's fault rather than any inherent flaw in the adopted work pattern. The distinction that is still made between part-time and full-time staff – a legacy of the core–peripheral model of manpower planning – is all the more ironic since the gap in working practices between the two groups is narrowing each year. Full-time staff working in cross-disciplinary teams with greater control over their work, in organisations which rely on output-based projects, are beginning to resemble job sharers or external contractors – and management methods designed to facilitate the work of part-timers are now providing a useful model for coordinating the activities of the entire workforce in lean organisations.

The FI Group, which pioneered methods to integrate and motivate a large part-time workforce in the 1980s, now employs a growing proportion of full-time staff. Yet as Mike Harling discovered when he joined FI in 1993 as director of human resources after 25 years with BP, the responsibility for work methods remains firmly in the hands of project teams still largely made up of home-based part-timers:

> I quickly discovered that performance at FI is output-based. We set very high quality standards from the centre and give project teams maximum support and maximum discretion in how these are followed. FI's quality standards are our control mechanism, not any complicated and costly form of direct supervision.

If Harling's comments seem commonplace it is because the working arrangements of the core workforce are moving closer to those of the periphery, not the other way around. The most appropriate management approach to project-based work in a delayered organisation is now well understood – less emphasis on telling, less assessing, less direct exercise of power, less focus on solo top-down leadership; more emphasis on achieving consensus, more involvement, more attention to information management, more focus on team-based, servant leadership.

What is often lacking is the behavioural shift needed to support this new role. Remember Christine Gaskell's comment: 'When changing culture, it is not enough to do things differently, you have to behave differently'? It is not surprising that most competency frameworks are designed to facilitate changes in behaviour and that one of the principal reasons is to close the glaring gap that often exists between the organisation's professed vision and its style of management. This was the focus of Rolls-Royce's competency framework and was also the focus of the framework adopted by the Hong Kong Government (see page 76).

Stakeholder management

The spotlight on the corporate governance procedures placed on UK companies by the Cadbury and Greenbury Reports has centred mainly on macro issues. The attention on the make up of not only the boards of publicly listed companies but also public sector bodies like NHS and police boards, schools and charities has helped to foster the philosophy that commercial organisations should be accountable not only to investors and funders but to customers, employees, national and local government, local communities and (where these are different from customers) direct users of products and services.

As we saw in the case-study of Rank Xerox (see Chapter 1), this has had a profound effect on the strategies and processes adopted by high growth companies. A new imperative is emerging which states that there should be no trade off between the interests and measured satisfaction of investors, customers and employees, and that there is a cause and effect relationship between the level of loyalty demonstrated to the organisation by all three.

However, stakeholder management has a micro dimension. The example on page 24 shows the extent to which project management in all organisations revolves around effective stakeholder management. With the spread of outsourcing and the TQM requirement that companies develop closer links with their suppliers and distributors, the stakeholders in almost any critical commercial project have become more numerous and the relationship with them more complex.

To take a further illustration, the manager of an outsourced accountancy department will have to manage the relationship with the staff undertaking the key functions – many of whom will have previously worked for the company which is now the client. He or she will also have to manage the expectations of senior management inside his or her own company, senior management inside the client company, representatives from what is left of the client company's internal accountancy function, and users of the outsourced accountancy function, for example creditors with outstanding invoices.

Research by Ashridge Management College in the 1980s (Geddes, 1987) suggests that it is usually the human and not the technical dimensions of project management that determine success or failure – providing yet another example of where the behavioural aspects of management, rather than professional knowledge or technical expertise, should be the leading criteria in any selection or development process.

Communications and relationship-building

Any discussion of stakeholder management leads very quickly to the importance of communications. The example, on page 78, of the company which contracted out its computer department only to discover later that a scam costing thousands of pounds had been going on to the certain knowledge of many of its former employees, who had been re-employed by the contractor, illustrates the potential exposure of organisations that engage in complex service agreeements for services that would have previously been undertaken in-house.

The growth in both the breadth and importance of a company's less immediate stakeholders – a direct result, we suggest, of the lean revolution – means that external communications are more complex involving a variety of publics with a different perspective of the organisation. Good communications will involve identifying the organisation's stakeholders, weighing and valuing their importance, and sustaining regular contact with them as part of a process of continuous improvement.

The HR function should be intimately involved in this process but often fails to be. A major crisis – such as that which occurred in Deutsche Morgan Grenfell over Nicola Horlick (see page 36) or happened to Perrier with their product withdrawal in 1990 – is likely to have a lasting impact on the company's ability to recruit and retain key staff at a time when loyalty needs to be constantly re-earned. The findings of the Roffey Park Management Institute survey on loyalty – that the reputation of the company is a critical factor in its ability to retain staff (Holbeche, 1994 and 1995) – merely confirms the conclusion of Charles Handy in the late 1980s that the most sought after professional and managerial staff will choose to work for organisations whose names will look best on their CVs. British Airways found this factor at work in its latest round of outsourcing when BA staff, offered the opportunity to work for the contractor taking over the catering service, demonstrated great reluctance to take up the option – not because the employment conditions were markedly worse than those they had enjoyed while working for British Airways but because they would no longer be working for a company that was a household name.

Womack himself argues that an important factor among individuals planning their careers is self-definition. Although he was referring to an individual's ability to field a creditable response to the question 'What do you do?' (at risk, Womack argues at a time when multi-skilling, cross-disciplinary working and portfolio management makes it increasingly difficult to come up with a pat one-line response), issues of self-definition equally apply in responding to the question 'Who do you work for?' As Linda Holbeche, author of the Roffey report, argues: in an age when frequent job moves are an accepted normality and recruiters expect candidates to have a varied CV, there is a thin dividing line in the minds of most professional and managerial staff between the benefits of building up a portfolio of professional experience with a variety of companies and those of developing an impressive internal career with one corporation. The issue does not just depend on the systematic career management they are offered by the company – although this is important – but on the extent to which the reputation of the corporation is sufficient to outweigh the benefits of moving around.

We have already argued on a number of occasions that the new generation of workers currently entering the labour market take it for granted they will have lots of different employers and frequent career changes. They have no emotional axe to grind about the seeming security of the past. Given that the 'employability contract' is a nebulous card for most organisations to play at the best of times (see page 86), the reputation of the company is probably its best asset in recruitment and retention terms. Building up the firm's brand equity, and in particular positioning it at the leading edge of events and developments in its industry, does not just secure investor and customer loyalty but the loyalty of the best graduates and professionals who want to benefit from the reflected glory.

More than opportunities for self-development, more than higher pay (unless you are offering packages well below the market rate), more than incentive schemes or company cars (an increasingly busted flush), the willingness of the individual to continue being associated with you is probably your most important retention tool. While closer links between the marketing, PR and HR departments was a brief manifestation of the late 1980s skills dearth, something more long-lasting is needed as firms enter the next phase of the lean revolution.

The active involvement of HR practitioners in corporate branding exercises aimed at all the organisation's stakeholders, providing active proof of the benefits of working for the organisation, should become standard practice. Tesco's HR function, for example, see the promotion of their own good personnel practice to the outside world as a priority. Recent coverage of Tesco's Excel graduate training programme is designed to show potential graduates that it is possible to develop a long-term career with the company across all sectors of the business, including gaining international experience. Roger Roberts, Tesco's director of personnel, comments:

> We are happy to promote our new approach to training because we are keen to show that Tesco is leading the field as a quality employer in the retail sector. Promotion of this kind is likely to become more important since our future expansion requires us to attract and retain high quality people well into the next century.

Turning to internal communications, HR practitioners should not just be participants; they should be pivotal. The experiences of Christine Gaskell at Rolls-Royce and Mike Dudding at Kent County Council illustrate the importance of the two-way communications role HR practitioners play in decentralised, delayered and devolved organisations: conveying the strategic purpose of restructuring and downsizing exercises, closing the gap between the employee's perception of the firm's vision and the practice, and sensing and diagnosing front-line problems.

An already sizeable armoury of tools and techniques, some old some new, are available to fulfil this role. We have seen that an employee survey conducted by MORI for a leading UK insurance company (see page 78) helped alert senior management to a hidden potential problem: while employees were more than satisfied with the employment conditions they enjoyed, there was a distinct lack of involvement which was undermining morale. Levi Strauss also used regular surveys to gauge whether staff felt that the company's commitment to fostering a balanced lifestyle among its employees was reflected in its terms and conditions (see page 68).

A number of companies employing TQM practices have also made better use of employee suggestion schemes. At Texas Instruments factories around the world, for example, the suggestion scheme is not cosmetic. It is an integral part of their total productive maintenance (TPM) programme which has devolved responsibility for maintaining and repairing automated manufacturing equipment to teams of operators anywhere from Europe to Asia Pacific. Supervisors and senior managers have a mandate to follow up suggestions (see Table 8); strict monitoring ensures that they do so.

Newsletters and house journals are being used more strategically. We have already seen that the inclusion of the activities of 'peripheral' staff plays a key role in making them feel more integrated into the organisation, particularly in terms of broadening their internal networks. Newsletters can also be used as the vehicle for motivational exercises designed to increase customer service and foster creativity. The Norwegian shipbuilding conglomerate Kvaerner, which has built up an increasing presence in Britain following its acquisition of Trafalgar House, uses a dedicated newsletter to help ideas circulate

Table 8 *Total productive maintenance (TPM) implementation concerns and actions at Texas Instruments*

Issues	**Actions taken**
Team meeting-rooms concerns	• Added additional small room for team meetings • Standardised TPM activity boards on the line wherein they can hold their meetings
Technical support attendance at the meeting was very poor	• Attendance tracking of technical support at the meeting • Technical support was given responsibility to lead or co-lead the team
Team cannot hold meeting due to workload	• Meetings are conducted outside the shift (on an overtime basis) • Meetings are being rescheduled within the week
High percentage of turnover	• Fast track TPM training for new hires • Adapted work appreciation programmes
Too many training programmes	• Tied up all related training programmes under a single initiative
Since TPM participation is mandatory some members feel that they are forced to be on the team	• TPM is tied up with the work cell approach wherein the emphasis is on team-based development • Regular review with the team to appraise/recognise participants
Teams receive training materials but methodologies are not being followed	• Revised all formats to be used by each team for standardisation process • Regular team reviews to ensure that the team follows the methodologies • Steps certification on autonomous maintenance activities

Issues	**Actions taken**
Good ideas are sometimes overlooked and not properly implemented	• Regular review of suggestion and implementation rate
Unproductive competition between teams	• Each group can choose its own theme or task to tackle, even with the same equipment
Confusion between teams	• Leadership/problem solving approach used to coordinate team activities

Source: Texas Instruments

and flow throughout the company through the use of competitions and 'ideas Olympics'.

The innovations that have resulted are generating substantial savings for the company. Welder Arne Svensson was awarded a prize of US$3,800 in 1991 for an idea on how to automate the welding of a key component which resulted in Kvaerner's subsidiary Kamfab's saving US$45,000 a year. A simple suggestion for an alteration to Kvaerner's pulping recovery boiler made by local administrator Anders Palmgren – changing the boiler's base plate from a rectangle to an octagon – has made the new unit cheaper and 15 per cent more efficient. Both individuals were awarded cash prizes but, equally importantly, were written up in double page spreads in a newsletter that is distributed to Kvaerner's worksites worldwide.

Significant opportunities exist to transfer much of this activity on-line. E-mail can be used through a modem from anywhere in the world. Inside a company it is likely to be on a corporate network. Between company locations it might take place across the Internet, through a leased line or through a traditional service provider such as CIX or Compuserve.

If the organisation is already highly wired, a further option is to set up a corporate *Intranet*. This can be used as an on-line library of company information – the company knowledge base or corporate memory, in effect. It can also be used by the HR department to disseminate key messages, information, surveys and points of discussion. Once it is published in the Intranet, anyone in the organisation with authorisation can have access.

The beauty of the Intranet approach is that it can be accessed from more or less any computer using one of the widely available Internet browser programmes. Effort and expenditure need to go into creating the Intranet information and putting it on the central computer but, because it is established only once, it is easier to maintain and control than distributed documents, which can quickly become outdated.

As we saw in Chapter 5, virtual communication has gone hand in hand with the lean revolution and feeds from the same culture of teamworking, cross-boundary collaboration and information free flow. By having information flow electronically, an organisation can achieve many of the objectives set out by Womack *et al.* in *The Machine That Changed the World* such as: eliminating unnecessary bureaucracy, slashing cycle times and bonding teams, even when they cannot spend much time together. Outside the company, even more benefit can accrue from electronic access to customers, suppliers and competitors across and within the Internet. If HR functions have not yet come to grips with the possibilities, they soon will.

7

Summary of Findings

The relationship between leanness and downsizing

- Leanness as a management concept is not synonymous with downsizing. Much of the downsizing in recent years has not been connected in any way with a systematic drive for improvement and quality by eliminating unnecessary processes and realigning essential ones. Rather it has been either an act of desperation by companies whose business is shrinking or, increasingly, a calculated act by commercially successful companies who want to remain successful by keeping costs down.
- The early processes of achieving a 'lean' organisation may involve jobs cuts – but not as a matter of course. Streamlining key processes and devolving responsibility to the front line can be achieved without losing any employees. Furthermore lean production, as defined by Professor Womack of the Massachusetts Institute of Technology, the originator of the term, was intended as an instrument for growth not contraction. Having reached the point where fewer employees are needed to get the same number of products to customers, he argues that companies should use this efficiency to speed up product development and find new markets – not to lay off workers and profit from the saving.
- Unless there are clear and immediate reasons, which can be justified to the workforce, continuous downsizing undermines the basic purpose of lean production techniques. The process of creating cross-functional teamwork and project management can only work with the active cooperation of the workforce and this is hardly likely to be forthcoming when management is asking employees to cooperate in eliminating their livelihoods.

The motivation behind leanness and its likely impact on the HR function

- Partly because Womack's theories of lean production were based uniquely on the strategies of Japanese car manufacturers, with an emphasis on mass manufacturing, the theory has spread piecemeal to other industries. There is little consensus about what 'leanness' actually means. Examining lean ways of working across a wide range of sectors, however, three reasons for taking up the concept stand out, each with fundamental implications for the role of the HR function.

- The first is the use of leanness to cut costs. Here the motivation is to keep the company competitive by continually keeping costs down, partially influenced by the short-term pressures imposed by institutional investors. The main concepts used are downsizing, restructuring and outsourcing. The role of the HR function is often one of 'kindly executioner' and 'paymaster of mercenaries'. Morale in the HR function is often low and there is little appreciation of their contribution by senior management.
- The second is the use of leanness to promote efficiency. At the lower end of this category, there is an emphasis on cost-based efficiency. The main concept used here is the old 1980s 'core–periphery' manpower model where a small core of firm-specific staff is supported by a periphery of flexible part-timers, contract workers and temporary staff that can be increased or decreased in line with the firm's economic performance. At the higher end of this category, there is an emphasis on market-led efficiency with organisations using various forms of process re-engineering to meet customer needs more quickly or more cheaply, or rapidly to respond to market changes. The role of the HR function is often one of 'systems administrator', designing and implementing appropriate resourcing strategies in response to a corporate plan that they have little or no role in influencing.
- The third is the use of leanness to support growth and innovation. At the lower end of this category there is an emphasis on total quality management, here BPR is combined with a company-wide philosophy of continuous improvement and values that place a premium on loyalty, recognition and empowerment. At the higher end of this category are organisations which use process redesign and value-based management to foster serendipity, bottom-up involvement, creativity and a free flow of ideas and information.

The HR function often plays a leading role in influencing and even proposing this strategy.

Organisational fitness and the HR practitioner as corporate physiologist

- The conclusion of the authors is that organisations should no longer strive to be lean – they should strive to be *fit*. In an age when innovation, creativity and knowledge management are essential to companies that want to maintain their competitive edge, a strategy which treats employees like any other resource – to be decreased and increased at will – makes little sense. Flexibility and leanness is important but only because it releases valuable human resources from unnecessary tasks to be redeployed where they are needed most.
- In this sense, the HR practitioner should act as the corporate physiologist. Just as a physiologist diagnoses an ailment or injury, comes up with a prognosis, prescribes a regime of care and observes its effect, so the HR practitioner conducts similar functions, in the case of both individual employees and, more strategically, with the organisation as a whole.

Issues for the future

- Whatever this book recommends, downsizing will continue. A growing number of organisations will engage in repeated blood-letting, not as an act of desperation but in a calculated attempt to remain competitive by keeping costs down. A continual pressure to reduce costs combined with a vital need to become more innovative means that firms will be put in the extraordinary position of being forced to continue the process of downsizing and outsourcing in one part of the organisation while simultaneously recruiting and motivating new staff in another. Recruitment and job cuts will often take place at the same time, and sometimes even in the same place, as posts filled by staff with outmoded skills are made redundant and posts requiring new skills that are often difficult to source materialise.

- Contrary to what many commentators claim, there is no large scale wish among the UK population for a return to permanent, full-time employment of the type we saw in the first three postwar decades. In addition to the unprecedented influx of women into the workforce, which has fuelled the demand for flexible working arrangements, a new generation of workers of both sexes is now entering the job market. These have no memory or expectation of 'traditional' working relationships. The workers that will matter most to employers – the ones that will add value to the company's operations – neither expect nor, in many cases, wish to remain in the same company for the rest of their working lives.
- What they will not abide is being led on. Organisations that hold out career prospects they know will not materialise, or hold out the prospect of skills and experience that will make the individual more employable without offering the opportunity for genuine self-development, help to breed a cynicism that is counterproductive to productivity, loyalty and morale.
- To cope with all these issues, HR practitioners have a key role to play in communicating the strategic purpose behind any restructuring, in advocating means to close the gap between the organisation's vision and its actual practice (for example in managerial styles, reward and recognition, and career development), and in fostering open and honest communication from the top down, founded on transparency and consultation.
- This role will be performed most effectively if the the HR communication strategy takes into account the 'virtual' network created by e-mail, discussional databases and the Intranet. This has created a network of 'brainwaves' that criss-cross conventional organisational boundaries, transcending even the new cross-functional framework created by lean stratregies. If the HR function learns to tap into this network rather than attempting to circumnavigate or suppress it, and uses the key figures in these networks to spread the good and bad news, it will be able to

disseminate information more effectively than by using more conventional outlets.

- Virtual networks also offer considerable scope for management education and development in lean organisations. A number of companies, working with leading business schools, have used project-based management programmes to strengthen the links between key communities in newly structured work units.
- Virtual networks are unlikely to supersede lean organisations. Effective computer-based communications are still most effective when founded on the tactile and tacit language provoked by face to face contact.

Developing an HR strategy for fitness

- Four business imperatives stand out if HR functions are to develop a coherent strategy to support the drive for organisational fitness.
- The first is behaviour. Organisations will only be able to respond to the needs of their customers and draw on the hidden talents of their workforce if their employees are sufficiently motivated and, in addition, able to demonstrate certain required types and standards of behaviour. Competency frameworks, if rigorously researched, have an important potential role to play in achieving this goal; so too do employee support and self-development programmes. The most effective 'lean' firms, however, redesign business processes to foster a free flow of ideas and information at all levels of the organisation.
- The second is the changing role of management. Three emerging roles are significant: interface management, to ensure that outsourced or outplaced services yield their maximum benefit; the management of flexible workers inside the firm, including the logistical task of managing reporting and monitoring procedures and the psychological aspects of induction and integration; and project and team management, which requires a shift in emphasis from direct supervision to consensus and 'servant' leadership.
- The third is stakeholder management. At a macro level this

requires organisations to make no trade offs between customer, investor and employee satisfaction; at a micro level project managers and team leaders will need to take into account the needs and expectations of a complex mix of stakeholders including team members, senior managers within their own firm, senior managers within a client firm, customers and users.

- The fourth is communications and relationship-building. HR practitioners need to become more involved in helping to shape and communicate their company's reputation and image, as part of a recruitment and retention strategy in a labour market where there is little residual loyalty. The HR function also needs to be the pivot in a continuous internal communications strategy, enabling them to communicate and clarify the strategic purpose of restructuring exercises, link the firm's vision and management practice more closely, and 'sense' and diagnose front-line problems. In this task, computer-based communications such e-mail, discussional databases and dedicated in-house Intranet systems are an important prospective tool for the future.

References and further reading

ATKINSON J. (1984) *Flexibility, Uncertainty and Manpower Management.* London, Institute for Employment Studies, Report No. 89.

BADEN-FULLER C. AND STOPFORD J. M. (1993) *Rejuvenating the Mature Business.* 2nd edn. London, Routledge.

BELBIN R. M. (1996) *The Coming Shape of Organization.* London, Butterworth Heinemann.

BERGGREN C. (1993) 'Lean production – the end of history?'. *Work, Employment and Society.* June. 163–88.

BREWSTER *et al.* (1990) *The Price Waterhouse–Cranfield Project on International Strategic Human Resource Management: Report of Findings.* 10–13.

CLARKE J, HOOPER C. AND NICHOLSON N. (1997) 'Reversal of fortune'. *People Management.* 20 March. 22–9.

CRUISE O'BRIEN C. (1995) 'Is trust a calculable asset?'. London Business School, *Business Strategy Review.* Vol. 6, No. 4.

GEDDES M. (1987) 'Project management: first find your leader.' *Manpower Policy and Practice.* Vol. 3, No. 1. Autumn. 13–16.

GERAINT J. (1996) 'Driving force' (a profile of Christine Gaskell, personnel director of Rolls-Royce Motor Cars). *People Management.* 25 July. 26–7.

HANDY, C. (1985) *The Future of Work.* London, Penguin.

HOLBECHE L. (1994) *Career Development in Flatter Structures: Report 1: Raising the issues.* Roffey Park Management Institute. August.

HOLBECHE L. (1995) *Career Development in Flatter Structures: Report 2: Organisational practices.* Roffey Park Management Institute. July.

HOWARD, R. (1992) 'The CEO as organisational architect: an interview with Xerox's Paul Allaire'. *Harvard Business Review.* September–October. 107–21.

INCOME DATA SERVICES (1995) 'Middle managers in transition'. *IDS Management Pay Review.* October. 19–22.

INDUSTRIAL RELATIONS SERVICES (1992) 'Lean production – and Rover's "New Deal"'. *IRS Employment Trends.* No. 514. June. 12–15.

INDUSTRIAL RELATIONS SERVICES (1993a) 'Restructuring for flexibility at British Airways Engineering'. *IRS Employment Trends.* No. 527. January. 12–15.

INDUSTRIAL RELATIONS SERVICES (1993b) 'TGWU's response to lean production at Rover'. *IRS Employment Trends.* No. 534. April. 5–7.

INDUSTRIAL RELATIONS SERVICES (1994a) 'Leyland Trucks: quality teams in gear'. *IRS Employment Trends.* No. 554. February. 13–16.

INDUSTRIAL RELATIONS SERVICES (1994b) 'Re-engineering industrial relations: from conflict to consultation at Barr & Stroud'. *IRS Employment Trends.* No. 555. March. 3–7.

INDUSTRIAL RELATIONS SERVICES (1995) 'Lean suppliers to lean producers: employee relations strategies'. *IRS Employment Trends.* No. 584. May. 11–16.

INSTITUTE OF MANAGEMENT (1996) *Are Managers Under Stress? – A survey of management morale.* Institute of Management. September.

INSTITUTE OF PERSONNEL AND DEVELOPMENT (1994) *Flexibility at Work in Europe.* London, IPD.

KETS DE VRIES M. AND BALAZS K. (1996) 'The human side of downsizing'. *European Management Journal.* April. 111–20.

KETTLEY P. (1995) *Is Flatter Better? Delayering the Management Hierarchy.* Institute for Employment Studies. IES Report No. 290.

KEUNING D. AND OPHEIJ W. (1994) *Delayering Organisations: How to beat bureaucracy and create a flexible and responsive organisation.* London, FT/Pitman Publishing.

KINNIE N. *et al.* (1996) *The People Management Implications of Leaner Ways of Working.* Issues series No. 15. London, Institute of Personnel and Development.

LAMMIMAN J., HOLBECHE L. AND SYRETT M. (1997) What Informs Decisions of Business Leaders. Roffey Park Management Institute. November.

LECKY-THOMPSON R. (1997) 'Tales of the City (HR in the Square Mile)'. *People Management.* 23 January. 22–7.

LEIGHTON P. (1990) *European Law: Its impact on UK employers.* London, Institute for Employment Studies. IES Report No. 156. October.

LEIGHTON P. AND SYRETT M. (1989) *New Work Patterns: Putting policy into practice.* London, Pitman Publishing.

LIDDLE R. (1996) 'David Blunkett from: Roger Liddle, Subject: the Social Chapter'. *New Statesman.* 15 November. 17.

MACLACHLAN R. AND OVERELL S. (1996) 'Public employers hit by working time rules'. *People Management.* 21 November. 8–9.

MCNERNEY D. (1996) 'HR adapts to continuous restructuring'. *HR Focus.* May. 4–6.

MERRICK N. (1995) 'Making the best of the daily grind' (flexible working practices at Rank Hovis). *People Management.* 31 May. 36–7.

MERRYMAN A. (1995) 'Downsizing: managing the pain and the gain'. *HR Focus.* December. 22–3.

MOSS KANTER R. (1989) *When Giants Learn to Dance.* New York, Simon and Schuster.

PURCELL J. AND HUTCHINSON S. (1996) 'Lean and mean?'. *People Management.* 10 October.

RAJAN A. (1994) *Winning People*. Centre for Research in Employment and Technology in Europe.
RAJAN A. (1998) *Tomorrow's People*. Centre for Research in Employment and Technology in Europe.
RAJAN A., VAN EUPEN P. AND JASPERS A. (1997) *Britain's Flexible Labour Market: What next?* Centre for Research in Employment and Technology in Europe.
REICHHELD F. F. (1996) *The Loyalty Effect: The hidden force behind growth, profits and lasting value*. Harvard Business School Press. March.
'The Response to "Lean Production"'. (1992) *European Industrial Relations Review* No. 223. August. 16–18.
ROTH S. (1995) 'Lean production in the German motor industry'. *P+European Participation Monitor*. Spring. 25–31.
SINETAR M. (1985) 'Entrepreneurs, chaos and creativity: can creative people survive a large company structure?'. *Sloan Management Review*. Winter.
SYRETT M. (1983) *Employing Job Sharers, Part-Timers and Temporary Staff*. London, Institute of Personnel and Development.
SYRETT M. (1994) *Competition, Effective Working and the Family: Making the connection*. International Year of the Family. October.
SYRETT M. (1995) 'The quest for quality: mastering management in Asia'. *Economist Intelligence Unit (Asia)*. August.
SYRETT M. (1997a) 'Goodbye to macho management'. *Director*. March. 49–55.
SYRETT M. (1997b) 'Changing the face of learning'. *Director*. April. 76–77.
SYRETT M. AND HOGG C. (1992) *Frontiers of Leadership*. Oxford, Blackwell.
SYRETT M. AND LAMMIMAN J. (1993) 'Deadly sins' (putting the learning organisation into practice). *Human Resources*. Autumn. 32–8.
SYRETT M. AND LAMMIMAN J. (1997) 'The art of conjuring ideas'. *Director*. April. 48–54.
THATCHER M. (1996) 'Networks create a professional buzz'. *People Management*. 29 August. 22–5.
'Time and a Half' (trends in working hours in Europe) (1996) *The Economist*. 24 August. 48.
'The Truth about the Social Chapter' (1995) *The Economist*. 9 December. 55–6.
VARLAAM C. *et al.* (1989) Skills Search: Television, Film and Video Industry Recruitment and Training Needs. Institute of Manpower Studies, IMS Report 171.
WALKER R. (1992) 'Rank Xerox – management revolution'. *Long Range Planning*. Vol. 25, No. 1. 9–21.
WOMACK J. (1996) 'The psychology of lean production'. *Applied Psychology: An International Review*. 119–52.

WOMACK J. AND JONES D. (1994) 'From lean production to the lean enterprise'. *Harvard Business Review*. March–April. 93–103.

WOMACK J. *et al.* (1990) *The Machine That Changed the World*. Rawson, Macmillan.

'Work to Rules' (European Union's working hours directive) (1996) *The Economist*. 16 November. 71.

WHITWORTH M. (1997) 'All of the day and all of the night' (UK employee working patterns). *Grocer.* 18 January. 50.

Index

Other titles in the Developing Strategies series

Managing the Mosaic
Diversity in action

Rajvinder Kandola
and Johanna Fullerton

Special Commendation winner at the 1995 Management Consultancies Association Book Awards.

Today, all organisations have to confront the challenge of diverse workforces. Yet many equal opportunity initiatives, in particular target-setting and positive action, which focus on specific groups such as women or ethnic minorities, are fundamentally flawed. To be effective, diversity strategies must tap into the talents of all staff, not just those from selected groups.

In this provocative but highly practical book, Rajvinder Kandola and Johanna Fullerton – chartered occupational psychologists at the Pearn Kandola practice in Oxford – set out to separate myth from reality. Drawing on a wide-ranging literature search, extensive experience of working within companies, and a survey of almost 300 organisations they give clear evidence that group-based equal opportunity policies are divisive and seldom successful.

Effective diversity strategies, pioneered by companies such as International Distillers and Vintners, are summed up in a detailed new model and linked to the ideal of the 'learning organisation', whose essential elements are flexibility, an empowering culture, universal benefits and business-related training for whoever needs it. Demographic changes, legislation, and increasingly globalised markets mean that diversity is now of central concern for all employers. This book provides definitive solutions to their problems.

Managing the Mosaic *makes a compelling case for the better management of the resources of the business: people with their wide variety of attributes, concerns, values and needs* – The judges' panel, 1995 MCA Book Awards

1994 200 pages Royal paperback ISBN 0 85292 556 5 **£18.95**

Leadership for Strategic Change

Christopher Ridgeway
and Brian Wallace

Effective strategic change leadership means seeing beyond day-to-day issues towards forging a new vision for the business. It means using influence to get others on board or facilitating them to achieve results. It also means choosing the right style – flexible, participative or more controlling – to adopt in specific circumstances.

This superb book enables potential change leaders to think through the issues, assess their core skills, put them into context and proceed to action. Stimulating questionnaires test for different kinds of leadership ability. Vivid case-studies spell out lessons in organisations that have undergone major change, and frank extended interviews with key players in change initiatives offer invaluable insights.

1996 240 pages Royal paperback ISBN 0 85292 613 8 **£18.95**

Ethical Leadership

Stephen Connock
and Ted Johns

Today's managers are constantly faced with acute ethical dilemmas; many may feel under pressure to sacrifice personal beliefs to corporate gain. Yet most books on business ethics are obscure and over-theoretical. This bold new text adopts a considered but completely practical approach that has nothing to do with saintliness and everything to do with organisational effectiveness and management action. Topics covered in depth, with stimulating company examples, include:

- balancing the needs and perspectives of different stakeholders
- codes of business conduct and common ethical issues about gifts, hospitality, confidentiality and conflicts of interest
- establishing the values to promote the right behaviour
- implementing core principles
- the roles of training and HR.

. . . a practical and inspiring definition of a contemporary ethical leadership and a businesslike explanation of why and how managers and organisations should use it – Occupational Safety and Health

1995 224 pages Royal paperback ISBN 0 85292 561 1 **£19.95**

The Communicating Organisation

Michael Blakstad and Aldwyn Cooper

Internal communication is not just part of PR or crisis management but a vital strategic tool. This pioneering book explains why employers need to devote more resources to this vital area. Drawing on their own consultancy experience, the authors reveal a number of fascinating case-studies, including:

- how the technology division of the Atomic Energy Authority carried out an in-depth audit and built its privatisation programme on the perceptions of people within, as well as outside
- how Price Waterhouse turned its consultancy skills on itself, forged a new philosophy, and communicated it to every employee
- how Meridian Broadcasting recruited its entire staff, moulded them into a single unit, and was on the air within 14 months of being granted a licence.

The text is written in a way which does not talk down to the reader . . . is well written and full of useful, well-grounded ideas – Organisations and People

The Power of Learning
A guide to gaining competitive advantage

Andrew Mayo
and Elizabeth Lank

Corporate survival depends crucially on adaptability, driven by employees willing and able continuously to update their knowledge and skills . . .

This bold and challenging book provides the vision and practical guidance to help all managers and directors to tap into the power of learning. Using real-life examples and a series of 'powerpoints' to enable companies to assess themselves, it shows how to:

- forge visionary, risk-taking leaders who can coach and empower others
- use the right language to promote a culture for learning
- support constant learning through people management processes – induction, performance management, career development and reward
- build an 'organisational brain' through information technology
- ensure all employees enhance their learning skills
- achieve maximum synergy in teams, networks, and communities
- break down the barriers to sharing information
- measure the added value of effective learning.

The book concludes with a practical self-assessment tool guaranteed to help companies of every size and sector set out on the journey to becoming more effective learning organisations.

1994 280 pages Royal paperback ISBN 0 85292 565 4 **£19.95**